WHY DOES MY BOSS HATE MY WRITING?

© 1999, 2007 by Becky Burckmyer

This 2007 edition published by Barnes & Noble, Inc.

ISBN-13: 978-7607-8942-1
ISBN-10: 0-7607-8942-8

Printed and bound in China

10 9 8 7 6 5 4 3 2 1

WHY DOES MY BOSS HATE MY WRITING?

Twenty-one questions smart business writers ask
before sending or printing

by Becky Burckmyer

BARNES & NOBLE

NEW YORK

TABLE OF CONTENTS

INTRODUCTION   VII

CHAPTER 1:   1
    Have I Written for My Audience?

CHAPTER 2:   12
    Have I Organized Properly?

CHAPTER 3:   23
    Have I Used a Tone That Will Appeal
    to My Reader?

CHAPTER 4:   39
    Have I Respected the Business E-mail
    Difference?

CHAPTER 5:   45
    Have I Preferred Active to Passive Verbs?

CHAPTER 6:   52
    Have I Used the Right Word?

CHAPTER 7:   68
    Do I Have Too Many Words?

CHAPTER 8:   76
    Have I Spiced My Writing with Variety?

CHAPTER 9:   82
    When All's Said and Done, Have I
    Avoided Clichés to the Nth Degree?

CHAPTER 10:   86
    Have I Created Unintentional "Noise"?

CHAPTER 11:   90
    Have I Venerated the Sacred Cows
    of Writing?

CHAPTER 12:   97
    Have I Dealt Carefully with Pronouns?

CHAPTER 13:   108
    Am I Making Bad or Good Use of
    Repetition?

CHAPTER 14:   113
    Have I Used Parallel Construction
    for Correctness and Charm?

CHAPTER 15:   120
    What's My OQ (Offense Quotient)?

CHAPTER 16:   128
    Have I Maintained the Subject-Verb
    Connection?

CHAPTER 17:   133
    Have I Addressed Issues of Agreement?

CHAPTER 18:   146
    Have I Used Punctuation As a
    Guide to Meaning?

CHAPTER 19:
    Have I Chosen Concrete Language
    Whenever Possible?   173

CHAPTER 20:
    Have I Been Ambiguous, Illogical, or
    Off the Wall?   179

CHAPTER 21:
    Have I Sweated the Small Stuff?   190

APPENDIX A:
    Getting Started and Following Through
    on a Writing Project   203

APPENDIX B:
    Numbers: the Basic Rules   212

APPENDIX C:
    A Word About Your PC   221

APPENDIX D:
    A Special Situation: Responding
    to Customer Complaint Letters   227

APPENDIX E:
    Memo and Letter Tips and Formats   236

APPENDIX F:
    Other Books on Writing   243

INDEX   251

INTRODUCTION

This book is for you if you're having trouble in your writing at work. It's also for you if you're the boss and you know something's wrong with the piece of writing that arrived on your desk this morning, but you can't put your finger on exactly what's the matter.

Those of you having trouble writing: I empathize. For most of us, writing is an extension of ourselves. It's personal, and criticism is painful. I should know: as an editor, I can't even e-mail a lunch invitation without getting blue-penciled, and it smarts amazingly. This book will teach you how to improve your writing and avoid the worst of the criticism.

Bosses: I empathize. I read lots of writing that needs help. And often it's very hard to zero in on what's wrong. This book will enable you to criticize objectively and helpfully—unlike the boss in the following True Horror Story.

A bank senior vice president in a large company once asked me to present a series of writing seminars targeted to upper management, herself included. Because I knew she was a good writer, I asked why she felt she needed help. She replied that her boss had become increasingly critical of her writing. She went on to describe his latest way of expressing his feelings. She had put a memo on his desk for his review and returned from lunch to find the memo on her desk—in a hundred tiny pieces. He had shredded it. After agreeing this didn't qualify as constructive criticism, we said bad things about him for a while, then planned the course. Later I got to thinking.

If you're like many people, though your writing may not literally get torn to pieces, your boss or manager may be returning it for rewrite with similarly unhelpful or inadequate explanations. You may get such vague comments as "It seems wordy," or "The language just isn't right," or if someone's been reading *The One-Minute Manager*, "I think you've got a good start here," meaning, "It's awful."

I've written this book to try to help. The chapters that follow lay bare what experience has convinced me are the 21 most annoying mistakes you can make in business writing. At the end of each chapter a feature called **The Bottom Line** reminds you in a few words what the chapter was about.

Most people in the business world are under too much time pressure to pause, review the rules of good writing, then practice them faithfully as they churn out e-mails, letters, memos, and reports. It's just not realistic. Yet for most people nowadays, writing well is not automatic. They start at the wrong end of the story; their mechanics—grammar, punctuation, treatment of capital letters and numbers—are not well founded; and they commit errors of style and coherence. Unfortunately, such writing can distract and alienate readers. Particularly discriminating readers, who can take a dislike to what you say because of the way you say it, and move on to assail, slash, and burn the *content* of your work. This is particularly true if you have a manager who has an intense personal relationship with grammar and style. A number of them do, and that shouldn't surprise us: good writing helps you get to *be* a manager.

If you're uncomfortable in the business writing you do, this book offers a solution. Go ahead and write: get it all down on your screen as fast as you can. Then run through this "21-Step Program," which effectively makes you a copyeditor for your own work. You can use The Bottom Line at the end of each chapter as a quick reminder.

Why Does My Boss Hate My Writing? will give you a fact-centered, measurable way to go back and make your piece of writing convincing, communicative, and free of faults. Everyone needs to do this. Yes, even if you *are* under a lot of pressure. We all are: but this will take very little time, and it's quality time, well worth it.

The questions that follow target the 21 most jarring problems of style, tone, grammar and punctuation, and appearance with which I have become familiar in my work as a business writer, editor, and teacher. I didn't say the most important. Some of the errors are major, others are very small, but *all* of them will make your boss and anyone else who reads your writing hate it. These 21 chapters highlight the errors that readers of all kinds—from company executives to customers—tell me again and again really bother them. There's a lot to be said for writing *defensively*: that is, not bothering people. You don't even want to make your reader aware of the act of reading because of something that jolts or distracts. Accordingly, the act of writing should be as seamless as possible.

I don't pretend this book tells you everything. It's not designed for beginners, although someone with poor writing skills would benefit from reading it. If you're in trouble with the basics (what is a sentence, what is a subject, etc.), you need a comprehensive style manual and the time to research it: I've listed my favorites for you in Appendix F. But I guarantee that if you work through the 21 questions, your writing will dramatically improve.

I realize nobody likes revising. The word has the smack of sincere and major tedium. But I think as you work with these questions, you won't feel as if you're revising, which is abstract and hard. You'll simply be running through a series of steps, which is concrete and easy.

I hope you're not getting harassment at the memo-shredding level. But if your manager, client, or colleague isn't satisfied with your writing, bang out your first drafts, then whip through this book before you print your final copy or send your e-mail. You'll quickly learn which questions tend to trip you up and which ones you effortlessly get right. From first draft to finished product will become a quick and easy progression. You'll discover the faultfinders simmer down as their confidence in you rises. And you'll gain confidence in your writing ability as well.

If you're a manager, take a look at *Why Does My Boss Hate My Writing?* I suspect you'll find these chapters pick up on the issues that concern you in the writing your people do. You'll be able to recognize errors easily and deliver criticism objectively. And once you've identified and labeled specific problems that recur, you're 90 percent of the way toward eradicating them.

Finally, a word to everyone: just be thankful if English is your native language, or if you learned it before your cortical layer (or wherever we store language) hardened. Experts tell us English is incredibly difficult to learn, and I believe it. A Japanese student in one of my business writing seminars asked, "Is the plural of 'horsepower' 'horsepowers' or 'horsespower'?" See? It could be a whole lot worse.

If your boss isn't happy with your writing, read the book through first so you understand each of the questions. Then begin using it: simply scan the bold type and be sure you've dealt with the issues before you send or print. Good luck! I hope you enjoy *Why Does My Boss Hate My Writing?* and find it helpful.

CHAPTER 1

HAVE I WRITTEN FOR MY AUDIENCE?

In their classic for college students, *The Elements of Style*, William Strunk and his prize pupil E. B. White give the best writing advice you can get for $8.95 (or whatever it now costs: it's more than worth it). Probably the most important single rule they offer is "Write for your reader." The advice sounds simple—like E.B. White's writing, deceptively so. Writing for your reader has many facets, and if you fail to bear them in mind, not only your boss but everyone who reads your writing will hate it. Don't let this happen to you. To write for your reader means the following:

☞ **Look through the reader's eyes.** First, it means seeing from the *reader's point of view*. Not a natural move, actually. When we write, we're intuitively focused our own feelings, responses, and viewpoints. We're eager to bring people round to seeing things as we do. But believe me, when you are writing in hopes of pleasing, convincing, or otherwise capturing readers, it is no time to be selfish. Resist the temptation, realizing that for the reader, the *reader's* point of view is paramount. True to human nature, most readers are at least subconsciously asking themselves some version of the question, "What does this have to do with me?" or "Why is this writer writing this to me?" or the still more basic cry from the interior, "What's *in it* for me?" So, to paraphrase John F. Kennedy, ask not what your reader can do for you, but what you can do for your reader.

How can you tell whether you are looking at your message from the reader's point of view? This is not really hard. Just ask yourself what effect this news will have on the person. If it's beneficial—we're offering you a better price, we're sending you a check, we're improving service—bring it out. Run it to the left-hand margin of your first line. Make it sharp, brilliant if you can. That's the hook with which you snag the reader:

Dear John:
Good news! Bergstrom has awarded you the contract to develop the 40 acres adjoining Route 2 as a high-end housing complex. I enclose, for your signature…

Dear Mr. Jones:
We're delighted to report your X-rays show no sign of any tumorous growth. At this point, we can conservatively say you are in remission and can reasonably anticipate no recurrence of…

Dear Ms. Carey:
Congratulations! you scored a nearly perfect 99 on your exam. This outstanding score qualifies you for advanced placement in Dr. Johnson's seminar next semester as well as…

> Dear Ms. Tuttle:
> Our records show you are correct: CountyBank inadvertently debited your checking account for a check drawn on your mother-in-law's account. Please accept our apologies and the enclosed receipt, which credits your account in the amount of...

If, on the other hand, your news will have a negative impact on the reader, your task is to be sensitive. That means you probably shouldn't lead off with it—smacking the reader in the face, as it were, with your bad news. Suppose, for example, you need to tell Mrs. J that she didn't get the job she wanted with your company. Here's how *not* to do it:

> Dear Mrs. J:
> We're sorry, but the programming job went to another applicant. We rejected your application for these reasons.

Pushing the bad news to the fore is hurtful and makes for a painful read. You don't want to do this to your reader—not only because it isn't nice, but because it makes better business sense not to go around creating pain, which can translate into antagonism. Who knows? you might want to hire Mrs. J in another capacity. Or maybe your first applicant says no, and Mrs. J begins to look better. Very few of us are powerful and autonomous enough to go around alienating people without considering the consequences.

> Dear Mrs. J:
> Thank you for submitting your application for the programming job. As it turned out, we had a tremendous number of applicants for the position, many of them with advanced courses and years of experience behind them. We must therefore…

Yes, she sees it coming. But at least she's being let down gently and politely. That's your responsibility as a writer.

But there's another good reason not to push bad news up front. It can cause your reader to ignore the rest of your message, even though it may contain an explanation, helpful advice, or possibly good news. Here's an illustration that I wouldn't believe if it hadn't happened under my own roof. As a high school senior, our son Charlie received a letter from ST University that began like this:

> Dear Charles:
> We are sorry to tell you that…

"Didn't get into STU, Mom," said Charlie, who had luckily been accepted where he'd hoped to go. He tossed the letter onto the pile of paper under which we think he has a desk. It surfaced six months later while I was looking for something else, and idly I scanned it. Of course you can guess what's coming. Somewhere around the fifth paragraph, below the fold, I read:

> If you are interested in entering STU in January,

> we would be pleased to have you. However, we need
> to know your decision immediately…

Moral: always finish reading a letter. But my point here is that STU had in fact *accepted* Charlie, and we didn't even know it. It didn't happen to matter all that much to us—but to someone else, it might have made a tremendous difference.

Sadly, this letter, a form doubtless sent to many applicants, could serve as a monument to writer-centered organization. Rather than considering what the reader needs to know or wants to hear, the writer has heedlessly spilled out the facts, probably in the order in which they came to mind. Reward: not only writing that hurts, but a total failure to communicate.

☞ **Watch your level.** Second, writing for your reader means *hitting the reader's level.* Your writing must be targeted to audience level in two ways. It must tap readers' level of *education.* Are you writing to high school graduates? College graduates? Grocers? Doctors? Teachers? It makes a difference. If you know to whom you are writing—at least predominantly—be sure your syntax, vocabulary, and length and complexity of sentences are geared to match.

Your writing must also tap readers' level of *knowledge.* In your occupation, avocation, and/or profession, you have probably already attained what I call the Dangerous Level of Knowledge, or DLK: you have become an insider. Your readers, on the outside, may or may not be as knowledgeable as you are. I use the word "dangerous" because when we become experts, we're no longer easily able to distinguish what others don't know. As a result, we risk failing to convey our message to readers. That's dangerous for everybody.

At the simplest levels, if you forget about the DLK, you may write elliptically: you leave out something—because it's self-evident to you—that is crucial to making your message clear to an outsider:

> Dear John:
> I look forward to meeting you on Friday morning, as you suggested, although of course Maureen won't be available to join us at that time.

Of course. Hello? Our writer neglected to consider that John didn't know, when he suggested a Friday meeting, that Maureen meets with senior staff every Friday morning.

Familiarity breeds contretemps unless you're on guard against the DLK.

It gets more complex than that, of course. Consider this, which I stole, almost verbatim, from a local bank's direct-mail copy:

> And here's the best news of all. When you're a CountyBank customer, you can attach your accounts and waive normal monthly service charges!

The writer was trying to say that the CountyBank customer could request that funds in a number of deposit accounts—checking, savings, certificates of deposit, IRAs—be added together each month to show a single balance on one monthly statement. If that balance was high enough, the customer wouldn't have to pay a service charge that month. Unfortunately, the DLK got in the way of communication. So familiar to the writer was this fund-pooling arrangement that she assumed her readers were also. Easy to see in someone else's work: hard to see in your own.

For that matter, when it comes to jargon, it's a minefield of DLK out there. Tread carefully. Jargon is incredibly useful: it's insider language, shorthand that lets people in a particular field talk quickly and easily to one another. But it doesn't fly outside the field. Listen to the software folks discuss URLs and GUIs—you'd think you were in a nursery, or maybe in Turkey. This language is beyond many people's understanding, not because it's so hard but simply because they haven't been exposed to it. Think about it. When you got on a computer for the first time, you didn't know what software, or a spreadsheet, or default formatting was. Stock analysts had to learn the meaning of puts and calls, selling short, buying on margin, and trading commodities. Financiers weren't born knowing the terms convertible debentures and diluted equity. Doctors learned to say multiinfarct dementia and rhinitis. All these specialists are at risk of forgetting they're using insider talk and laying it on generalists—and doubtless so are you. Because of the DLK, we forget. And of course, as surely as if we try to write Portuguese to Greeks, we will fail to get our message across.

To be sure you've addressed the DLK, pretend your mother, your child, your spouse, or your carpool mate is reading what you've written. Could he or she understand it? You can actually visit or phone the person and read selected lines. (Works for me. And gives my mother a chance to update me on her "other" grandchildren—the well-behaved, clean ones.)

You can also take a cue from the *Wall Street Journal*, highly respected in business circles. It's because of the DLK that the *Wall Street Journal* never writes "IBM" without including the information that IBM is an abbreviation for International Business Machines. It usually adds a helpful identification tag line as well, such as "the computer giant"—just in case there's one person, even one, in America—I picture Rip Van Winkle waking from his 20 years' nap and reaching for the stock market page—who's unfamiliar with Big Blue. Now the *Wall Street Journal* has as well-educated and homogeneous a population as any newspaper in the country. If its writers are told to pitch, as I've heard they are, to "a bright but ignorant reader," it's surely appropriate for us to do the same. Identify; explain; describe.

Don't worry that you'll sound simplistic or condescending if you write to edit out the DLK. Business writing today is so information intensive that your readers will be happy to "cruise" past your explanation of a procedure, or definition of a word, they already know. It gives them a breather. As an editor, I notice no one ever calls me up and says, "I'm sending you a piece that's easy to understand, and I'd like you to make it harder."

Remember also that "your reader" may include a wider audience than you imagined. So imagine this audience. Is your boss, for example, likely to send your memo up the chain? Often the top brass are less familiar with a particular area of expertise and its jargon than you might think. They have a lot of areas to manage, and it tends to make them generalists. But because they don't like to admit that they don't understand, they feel uncomfortable, and they take it out on your copy. You don't want that. You want them to *like* what you've written.

☞ **Use "I" advisedly.** Finally, and I want to go carefully here, writing for your reader means in one sense cultivating the word *you* at the expense of *I.* In one sense. I am *not* suggesting you get rid of a personal pronoun we all need and one that can add importantly to your tone. Many people writing today apparently learned from some Draconian fourth-grade teacher (when I find her, I want words with her) that *I* is always inappropriate in business writing. Good grief. As if communication weren't already impersonal enough, with printers spitting out mass mailings directed to "Customer," telephone calls reduced to a series of typing exercises on the keypad, and children linked to home only by e-mail or fiscal shortfalls. To members of a culture increasingly driven by mindless technology, *I* can come as a welcome surprise. At the very least, it means there's someone in there. So I don't want you to engage in witch-hunts against the vertical pronoun. I simply want to raise your consciousness so you can watch for *I* as a flag that may—though it may not—signal a miscarriage of emphasis.

When you've written *I,* particularly in multiples, ask yourself whether its use is justified. Do you have a role? Why are you in there? Perhaps for a very good reason—for example, because you are responding to a letter originally written to someone else.

Dear Mr. Smith:

Thank you for taking the time to write Mr. Bergonzi, Croftman's CEO, with your suggestions for improving service to Croftman's Lynnfield customers. Mr. Bergonzi asked me to respond to your thoughtful letter, as I am the senior vice president responsible for customer relations in the Northeast Region, which includes Lynnfield.

Mr. Smith needs to know why he's hearing from you, rather than the CEO, and will be gratified that you're at a senior management level. Hence the information pertaining to you is relevant, and the references to yourself are appropriate.

You may also be taking it upon yourself to apologize for a glitch made by your company.

> Dear Mrs. Townsend:
> I apologize, on behalf of Macy's, for the inconvenience you experienced when the store neglected to remove the ink cartridge from your newly purchased evening dress. I fully agree that the fault rests with the store, and we will fully compensate you for the loss of the gown. If I could compensate you for an occasion thoroughly spoiled, I would do that as well. It is unfortunate that the King of Sweden proved so aggressive in his efforts to remove the cartridge, as its explosion surely ruined the Nobel Ball for you. Again, my apologies. I have credited your account for the full price of the dress.

Note the frequency with which the personal pronoun appears in this letter. It functions here to underscore the good faith of the company towards the customer and to assure her that a sympathetic person has heard, understood, and (to the extent possible) addressed her complaint. That's a worthy *I* message.

If none of these reasons apply, you may have written an *un*worthy *I* message—one that reflects an inflated sense of self-esteem—or appears to, which is just as bad. At the very least, though it's probably accidental, it's writer, not reader, centered.

If you've identified an unworthy *I* message, see whether you can rephrase your sentence using the pronoun *you.* You get points for every *I* removed and *you* inserted.

> "I" message: I hope I have explained this matter satisfactorily. If not, I'll be happy to go over it again.

> "You" message: If you would like a fuller explanation, you are welcome to call me anytime at 968-642-7777.

The pleasant tone is there in each case, but the *you* spin brings it out.

Target your readers accurately so they'll understand what you're trying to tell them.

—— THE BOTTOM LINE ——

- **Look through your reader's eyes.**

- **Watch your level: how much do your readers know and understand?**

- **Use *I* carefully, liberally blended with *you.***

CHAPTER 2

HAVE I ORGANIZED PROPERLY?

Here's the one that drives the most bosses up the most walls. A study of Fortune 500 companies confirmed what you may already have discovered: lack of organization is the biggest complaint managers have about the writing of their subordinates.

We continue to focus on your audience in dealing with proper organization, which sounds hard but is really easy: To organize your writing well, all you really need to do is place the message in one of two categories: news that's *good or neutral* from the reader's point of view, and news that is *bad* from the reader's point of view. For good or neutral news, organize by the *Big Top* method. For bad news, use the *Rock Bottom* method.

The Big Top is the *deductive* method of reasoning: from the major premise to the fine points. In Latin, the prefix *de-* means, among other things, "down from." This method is sometimes called the inverted pyramid: big idea on top, smaller and smaller details tapering to the finish.

☞ **The Big Top method.** This means putting your main idea first. In the first line, actually. Busy people tend not to read every word of a document. They scan. That's how President Kennedy could read an impossible number of newspapers at breakfast. (I read about this in Theodore Sorenson's biography, *Kennedy*, and lost count at 14.) What do they scan? The top line, left margin of every paragraph, that's what. Sometimes just the top line of the *first* paragraph, actually, and perhaps the last.

So if you have factual or neutral news—information—make it easy for the reader to get the gist. And if you have good news—you're offering a job, awarding a contract, approving a loan, showcase it. Run it up front where the lucky reader can see it and be glad. Remember the hypothetical question: "Why this communication?" Your first sentence in such cases should answer this question.

Here's an example of an opening for a good news letter:

> Dear Mrs. Shurcliff:
> We agree you were overcharged for the new oil burner and installation and have enclosed a check that reflects the difference between the price we initially quoted you and the amount for which you were billed and which Mr. Shurcliff paid.

Here's another, this time the opener for an e-mail containing neutral news:

> FROM: Max Blaustein <mblaustein@regalinc.com>
> TO: All Regal Associates <assoclist@regalinc.com>
> SUBJECT: Insurance Benefit Information
> Session May 4

> DATE: April 24, 20__
>
> You are invited to an all-day information session in the Cronley Auditorium on May 4 from 8:00 a.m. until 5:30 p.m. Representatives of our carrier companies will speak and answer your questions. We hope everyone will be able to attend, as some of our benefit offerings have changed. Please mark the date on your calendars.

On the subject of memos, e-mail or paper by the way, extend the Big Top principle into the heading—the subject, or RE: line. Make it very descriptive, like the one above—not a title, but a headline. Not *Gone with the Wind*, in other words, but "Spirited Antebellum Belle Dressed in Draperies Survives War of Northern Aggression." Not *The Firm*, but "Up-and-Coming Memphis Attorney Uncovers Organized Crime Activity." You get the idea.

You can refine on the Big Top method to make it easier for the reader to absorb your message. Particularly in a complex paragraph or piece, if you want to reinforce your main idea, you can restate it at the end. You can also explain or amplify what you mean in the second sentence. Or both. Here's a simplistic example:

> Jim Sandefur is an excellent developmental editor. Rather than simply correcting errors in syntax or spelling, he revises a writer's copy so that it makes sense and is effective and pleasant to read. He does not

(TOPIC SENTENCE)

(AMPLIFICATION)

hesitate to tackle complex financial management tracts and even technical writing. His clients over the past seven years include Curzon University, novelist Jane Burrows, the law firm of Polk and Maddux, and MacroFine software development. All of them sing his praises. He is arguably the finest developmental editor in this area.

(SPECIFIC DETAIL SUPPORTING TOPIC SENTENCE)

(RESTATEMENT OF TOPIC)

The Big Top method is the way Mrs. Prentiss taught you to write a paragraph back in sixth grade: a topic sentence and supporting details. It works not only for a paragraph, but for a writing project as a whole.

A newspaper article is a good example of the Big Top method. The headline tells you what the entire story will be about: "President Bush unveils crime plan." The rest of the article, if it's a good article, tells you what the president plans to do about crime. No more, no less. Within the article, each paragraph begins with a topic sentence that tells you what that paragraph is about: "The president outlined his plans to tackle juvenile crime…"; "The plan calls for $200 million to be spent…"; even "The president hinted at future plans to…" You can scan the topic sentences and decide what you want to read about in detail.

But be careful. Faced with a blank page, especially if you're under serious time pressure (and we usually are), it's also easy to default to another mode of organizing: telling your story as it happened, from beginning to end. This is called, among other things, the chronological or lab report method. It's quick and easy writing, because it doesn't require much brainwork: all you have to do is remember the order of events, transcribe them, and you've got yourself a story. Alas, this slipshod method is usually only too evident—and as Samuel Johnson wrote, "What is written without effort is in general read without pleasure." If you use this primitive *modus operandi* for anything but a first draft, it is likely to flop.

Here, for example, is a paragraph that tracks events chronologically:

> On January 2, John was given the task of developing the fiscal-year business plan for Amtex. After working on it for two months, he presented it at the Amtex board meeting in March. The chairman of the board and various members asked a number of questions about cost, time frame, and management realignments, which he was able to answer to their satisfaction. Ultimately, the board unanimously approved the plan, effective immediately.

Well, the author walked us right through John's story from the beginning to the end, and what a dull, dumb story it was. Why is it so dumb and dull? Because priority has been assigned solely on the basis of *when* things happened, not on their relative importance. The reader must wait till the last sentence before the really significant information, the approval of the plan, emerges. The walk-through works well with stories that begin "Once upon a time," but you're not the Brothers Grimm, nor are you dealing with that level of reader involvement. Rather than waiting with bated breath for you to come to the point, your readers may simply stop reading. Why not? They can't see what you're driving at. Or if you're driving at anything.

In these latter days of shortened sound bites and diminishing attention spans, the prize goes to the person who spits the message out first. So if you've got something to say, say it. Jam the essentials into the first line, right up against that left-hand margin, In most cases, this means ignoring chronology and leading instead with what is actually in most cases the conclusion, or the result. In your end is your beginning, as it were, like that snake with its tail in its mouth.

Here's the paragraph on John's business plan, reorganized on the Big Top principle:

> We will implement John's business plan immediately, after its approval yesterday by unanimous vote of the Amtex board of directors. The weeks of work he has put into the plan since he was given this responsibility January 2 paid off: he was able to answer the board's intensive questioning into the plan's provisions for cost, time frame, and management realignments to everyone's satisfaction.

Sometimes you may be asked to use the chronological method—for an update, for example. This doesn't prevent your inserting a two- or three-line recommendation or summary at the top. This effectively turns the piece into a Big Top document.

One writing student told me he didn't like to reveal his message deductively. He preferred to create suspense, he told me,

ignoring the cynicism deepening in my face. He aspired to lead
his readers along as he spun a web. Or something. Please, please
believe me, this technique will not work. In fact, it's a route to
self-destruction as a communicator. You are not writing a mys-
tery novel, nor doing the Dance of the Seven Veils. Put your
readers in the picture right away.

Now that I've told you how ineffective this method is for
good or neutral news, let me show you how well it works for
bad news.

☞ **The Rock Bottom method.** When you have to communicate bad news, you organize *in*ductively, which in Latin literally
means "leading in." You begin with the details and work toward
the conclusion. Rather than being positioned up front for maximum exposure, your bad-news message doesn't appear until
the end of the paragraph or piece. Here's an example of a paragraph that's organized on the Rock Bottom principle:

> Your performance during the past six months has
> been erratic. In fact, our clients have found it diffi-
> cult even to reach you, and that is understandable,
> as your schedule shows a record of absenteeism for
> a variety of reasons, none of them related to work.
> In addition, the documents you were charged with
> preparing have either not been completed or show
> evidence of having been hastily and sloppily put
> together. In view of these facts, I feel I have no
> choice but to place you on probationary status until
> your work improves.

Despite its chronological relating of events—from the start of the six months to the present—this paragraph is ideally organized, because the message is a negative one. The payoff is bad news. And for bad news we use the message-last approach. It's sometimes called the pyramid method: working from the little stuff to the big stuff. I call it Rock Bottom, picturing the reader receiving the bad news—the refusal, the summons, the chop—and feeling that this apocryphal location has been hit.

The advantages of the Rock Bottom method for conveying bad news are threefold. First, you cushion the blow by leading up to it. Consider a bad-news message such as this one, wrongly organized by the Big Top method:

> Sam—
> We can't let you go to the conference in Winchester. Senior staff met yesterday and decided you shouldn't go for the following reasons. First...

In your face with the bad news! This is rude, and it's insensitive. It's almost as if the writer enjoys being a bad hat: not a good message to send to subordinates or anyone else. In contrast, the inductive method, because it's indirect, can make you seem perhaps just a shade unwilling to break the news.

Second, you **build a case.** By the time your reader reaches the unwelcome conclusion, he or she at least understands why you came to it. You make your plea for the inevitability of the final blow.

Third, you **ensure you're heard.** If you slug the reader with your ugly message up front, he or she may well read no further. That's the way many people react to bad news. If you want to

be certain your entire message is read, you'd better Rock
Bottom it.

Finally, a few quick tricks for organizing that will improve
any piece:

☞ **Use "connective tissue" to show the direction of
your thinking.** We all want to omit *needless* words, but certain
words are critical to your meaning. Don't omit words such as *in
addition, however, although*, and *but*. These words are not there
just to connect gracefully. They perform an essential function in
showing your reader the relationship between what you've just
said and what you're about to say. The Dangerous Level of
Knowledge sometimes makes us think we don't need these
words. That's only because we already know the story. The
reader needs them. A lot. Consider:

> John says he thinks a takeover is highly unlikely. He
> is preparing a "poison pill" clause to help us protect
> ourselves in a takeover situation.

Without the magic word *although*, or *but*, or *however*, these two
sentences make no sense together. They contradict each other. I
won't belabor the obvious. Be free with your connective tissue: it
helps your reader follow the direction of your thinking. *However*
primes the brain for a contradiction. For readers who weren't paying close attention, it's also a signal to go back and make sure they
know what's about to be contradicted.

Again because of the Dangerous Level of Knowledge, I'm
strongly inclined to let my structure show: the "bones," or

underlying organizational principles. Consequently, I love words such as *first*, *second*, and *third*; phrases such as *in the past*, *in the present*, *in the future*. These not only show readers what you're driving at, but they also bring careless ones up short: if they arrive at *third*, for example, and realize they've already missed two points.

These words are powerful rhetorical devices that keep the reader abreast of your thinking.

☞ **Be true to your contract with the reader.** If you plan to discuss several items, list them in an order that you like. Then **follow that order**. Don't cite items 1, 2, and 3, then go on to discuss item 3 first. This is breaking an implied deal you've made with the reader. Let's say you're going to write about housing in the city, the suburbs, and rural areas. You craft a topic sentence that reads just about like that. Now that you've so ordered them, you are bound to discuss the city first. (And if you decide you'd rather talk about the suburbs first, reorder your topic sentence and put the suburbs first.)

☞ **Work from the easy to the difficult.** Follow this rule in a series of words or phrases, unless some other organizing principle is in effect:

> Your office furniture will include a desk, a credenza, and three five-drawer file cabinets.

The nature of the brain, to my (limited) understanding, is such that it appreciates receiving the simple item first, which "primes" it to understand the function of the more complex ones that follow. Makes sense to me, and it sounds good too: Mairzy doats, and doazy doats, and little lambsy divey. Fish nor fowl nor good red herring. Gold, and myrrh, and frankincense. The Nina, the Pinta, and the Santa Maria. You get the idea.

☞ **Use bullets and numbering to clarify points.**
Remember that numbering gives you two benefits that the currently popular bullets don't: you set priorities with numbers, and you can identify a numbered item for reference. It's easy to refer to number 6, rather than to "the next-to-last, I'm sorry, next-to-*next-to*-last bullet."

Sound easy? It is.

——— THE BOTTOM LINE ———

- **Look through your reader's eyes.**

- **Use the Big Top Method (major point first) for good or neutral news.**

- **Use the Rock Bottom Method (major point last) for bad news.**

- **Show the direction of your thinking with connective tissue: however, therefore.**

- **Discuss points in the same order in which you introduce them: 1, 2, 3.**

- **Work from the easy to the difficult when listing a series of items.**

- **Use bullets and numbering for clarity.**

CHAPTER 3

HAVE I USED A TONE THAT WILL APPEAL TO MY READER?

The tone of a piece of writing is its overall mood: the writer's attitude toward the material and toward the reader. And it's extremely important. Remember "Don't look at me in that tone of voice!"? Tone is the key to your salability. It can help you convince the skeptical, pacify the irate, stroke the philanthropic, rally the uncommitted. By the same token, if you don't have tone elements under control, you can alienate readers.

The following rules will help you edit out tones that alienate. From time to time you may need to use them to punish a sinner or whatever: my aim here is to make sure you realize it when you use an off-putting tone. Because it infuses your entire message, tone is a powerful tool.

Here are some quick and easy ways to ensure a winning tone:

☞ **Edit out a negative point of view.** Most of us are problem solvers. Therefore, it's easy for us to fall into the trap of writing about what's wrong, what we can't promise, can't do, can't get. Most of the time, this is not a desirable tone. It 's easy to spot negative writing, once you're reminded. It tends, not sur-prisingly, to have a lot of negative words in it: words like *unfortunately*, *no*, *not*, *unable*, *impossible*, and anything that ends in *n't*. These are all words to edit out if you want a positive tone. *Fail*, *regret*, and *disappointment* are also near the top of my hit list.

Luckily, most negative writing can easily be recast in a positive form. If your work is stressing what isn't doable, try thinking positively and stressing what is:

> Negative: Our company does not deal with the public.
>
> Positive: Our company deals exclusively with distributors.
>
> Negative: We can't let you use the equipment on weekends.
>
> Positive: Feel free to use the equipment any weekday.
>
> Negative: We regret to inform you that you are currently ineligible for benefits.
>
> Positive: When you complete a waiting period, you'll be eligible for benefits.

It's like thinking of your latte cup as half full rather than half empty.

☞ **Edit out tentative writing.** Your reader seeks to learn from you. As a writer, you represent, in a sense, authority. If you couch your message in uncertain or shilly-shallying language, he or she will be uncertain whether you can be believed and trusted. Unless you have a particular reason to sound unsure of yourself, don't fall into these traps and lose reader confidence:

1. Using tentative verb forms. *Would*, *should*, and *could* are conditionals that can make you sound uncertain how your information will be received.

> No: If our proposal is accepted, we *would* implement a full-scale waterproofing of the dome.

> Yes: If our proposal is accepted, we *will* implement…(Or, thinking positively, *When* our…)

The same goes for the *-ing* verb form, or present participle. Use it sparingly and advisedly. There's a big difference in tone between the following two sentences:

> I am expecting your draft by tomorrow.
> I expect your draft by tomorrow.

On occasion, you may prefer the softer tone of the first, but be aware that's the tone *-ing* creates.

2. Littering your writing with qualifiers. Sometimes you have to. But when you sprinkle your writing with *a bit, rather, somewhat, to a certain degree,* and so forth, you appear to be sitting on the fence, hedging your bets, and covering your you-know-what. Not a nice picture, and it causes readers to lose faith—and who can blame them? For example:

> I am somewhat in favor of selling a little of the company's stock.

Well, are you or aren't you? You owe your reader, if possible, an unequivocal answer.

> I am confident it will benefit us to sell between 10,000 and 40,000 shares of company stock.

I'd like to point out one other aspect of this modifying business. If you modify strong adjectives, those descriptive words, you will come off sounding eccentric, or worse: to the extent the adjective is powerful in its own right, you will make yourself—I have to say it—ridiculous. I had a friend who used to insist on saying things were "very terrible." (Making matters worse, she was from Stony Creek, a rural hamlet of southwest Virginia, and she pronounced it something like "vurry turrible.") I couldn't persuade her not to say it, but I think I finally convinced her not to put it in writing. Here's an example in print from a company president and CEO:

> When [Phil] was talking to the board yesterday, he showed the market to book, a *relatively critical* number that is now hovering at 300 percent....

Either something's critical or it isn't. The stronger the descriptive word, the more foolish you appear when you modify it. Our CEO could have omitted *relatively* with no damage to his message. Similar words that I believe should never be modified include (there are plenty more, but you'll get the idea):

changeless	ironclad
correct	omnipotent
immovable	pregnant
irresistible	unique

So be careful with the modifiers. Don't compromise strong words with descriptive words that weaken them and make you look silly.

☞ **Edit out any suggestion of manipulation.** Two maneuvers to avoid so you don't appear to be turning on an artificial brand of charm to get your way. (You may certainly do that, but I don't want you to get caught doing it, and some moves are just too obvious.)

First, don't thank anyone in advance. It's hypocritical—how can you be grateful for something that hasn't taken place? It also indicates that you are quite sure your wishes will be followed, so it preempts free will on the reader's part.

> So that we may share our findings with the Board of Directors at the Annual Meeting, please have 20 copies of the satisfaction survey on my desk by 5:00 p.m. Thank you in advance for your attention to this matter.

Right. And you're not welcome.

Second, watch namedropping: don't keep using the reader's name in an e-mail message, memo, or letter:

> Jim, I hope I can count on your support.... Please let me hear from you, Jim, at your earliest convenience.... Jim, I look forward to meeting....

This ploy is intensely easy to overdo. And, partly because it's been overdone, a lot of people *really* don't like it, I among them. As a bond trader friend of mine who spends a lot of time with salesmen says, "I just can't stand to hear the sound of my own name ringing in my ears." It's pretty much the same in writing—except that in a face-to-face conversation the twitch of annoyance across your listener's features will tell you you are overdoing it. It's bad enough in a personal communication; it's even worse, I think, in a direct-mail piece, because everyone knows the names are input by brain-dead keypunch operators and spat out by computers:

> Bucky Bueckberger, you may have ALREADY won
> $1 million!!!!

(Now why would I be suspicious of this nice message?)

In primitive cultures, to know someone's name was to have the power of life and death over the person; therefore one's real name was a jealously guarded secret. Even in modern civilization, people's names are still essential parts of their being. So be careful how you toss a person's name around in your communications. To you it may appear a harmless stratagem, friendly and personal, but it can be perceived as an irritating, even controlling, maneuver to your reader. If you're still convinced namedropping will charm someone, go ahead, but at least limit yourself to just one drop per communication.

☞ **Edit out *unintentional* unkindness.** Occasionally a piece of writing must be harsh or unpleasant in tone. But too often people surprise me by writing—to an audience of customers, for example—in an appallingly unkind way. There's rarely an upside to writing unpleasantly to somebody up the chain from you, as customers are by definition. When challenged, my cruel and unusual writers are often amazed: they had no idea how they were coming across. A few suggestions to avoid writing that's unintentionally rough on your readers:

1. Watch generalizations that put people or groups down, directly or indirectly.

> MIT students are poor conversationalists outside their own fields of expertise.

> Wellesley women make good lawyers.

That second sentence will offend alumnae from six out of the former seven sister colleges, and any number of lawyers—many more than the Wellesley alumnae it will flatter. That's not even good business economics.

2. Edit out language that blames or belittles.

> If you had read the manual sent with your laser printer, you would not be experiencing a problem with sheet slippage.

> As you are surely aware, this seminar is available to corporate clients only.

> Most people realize that ABC is a closely held corporation.

3. Ditto language that patronizes or self-applauds at readers' expense.

We have a lot of experience helping people who can't grasp the basics of math.

A prestigious law firm such as Grad, Levy naturally receives many requests like yours.

Kindly send us a copy of your certification as a harbor pilot.

(If ever a word had overtones that belie its sound, the word is *kindly*, in the sense used above—sort of a one-word oxymoron. I never, ever use it.)

4. Check to be sure you haven't unwittingly expressed disbelief.

If, as you say, your contract stipulates services through the end of this year...

You seem to be suggesting that it is we who owe you money.

You claim that we sent your package on April 8.

Such sentences are necessary and appropriate on certain occasions—shortly before you go to court, perhaps. But the old definition of a gentleman is "One who never inflicts pain unintentionally." Don't

inflict pain by mistake in your writing. Strive to be a
person of gentility, as we say in these politically correct days (see Chapter 15).

☞ **Remove strained, overly formal, or outdated language.**
Relax already. Queen Victoria is no longer with us, and flowery
phrases have abdicated in favor of conversational language. (I said
conversational, not colloquial. Your business writing should pass
the read-aloud test, but it shouldn't sound as if you're talking
with your best friend. At least not the one who taught you to
swear.) This means you can dispense with

> Enclosed please find
> Hoping to hear from you, I remain
> I beg to remind you
> We deem it necessary
> As of even date herewith
> Pursuant to
> Inasmuch as
> Yours of the first inst. (whatever that is)

and similarly labored phrases. Pleading, begging, and deeming are
out, presumably for the count: try asking, suggesting, and believing.

☞ **When you must apologize, do it up front and in full.**
If, I mean when, you or your organization goofs—it's going to happen—admit it and say you're sorry, rather than trying to protect
yourself. The latter builds a defensive wall between you and the

reader. Besides, it lacks style. As somebody said about slipping on the ice, it's not the falling down that looks so bad, it's the effort not to. Trying not to apologize is much the same. It's not only ungraceful, though—it also isn't fair. If you owe, you should pay up. Besides, it's hard to stay mad with someone who is figuratively rolling over and putting four paws in the air. So apologize at the beginning of your message. Apologize profusely. If you have a rebate, or premium, or little present you can throw in, or a pile of money (heals many wounds) go ahead and do that too—just be sure your organization will back you up.

No: Evidently a mistake was made somewhere along the line. Two's Company regrets the occurrence. Complaints about our service are infrequent...

Yes: On behalf of Two's Company, I apologize for the error in your March billing and the inconvenience you experienced as a result. At Two's we try very hard to prevent such mistakes. Occasionally, they nonetheless do occur. We have credited your account with the amount of the overcharge...

☞ **If someone *else* goofed, don't whine about it.** Sometimes it's not your fault, it's the other guys'. Give them a break. It could have been you: we all make mistakes. Simply state the facts and ask for whatever apology or reparation you need. Don't drone on and on about how awful it was for you. Nobody likes a whiner, and nobody likes a martyr. Remember the parental lament, "After all I've done for you, this is the thanks I get"? Did it make you sorry, or just plain mad? Why compromise your relationship with the goofer? That only adds to the problem.

Here are two letters dealing with the same issue: a business broker has been referring inappropriate prospects as buyers for the writer's company. The first letter is subjective and emotional; the second, objective and factual.

Dear Steve:

Last week you showed my company to yet another window shopper who has neither the collateral to obtain financing nor any in-depth understanding of what it takes to run a business such as Wyziwhiz Works. In fact, I don't think Jack Smith understands what a printed circuit board is, let alone the complex issues involved in estimating a job, making the parts, assembling them, and getting them to the customer in a timely manner. You are taking up my time, of which I have so little nowadays, and with each person you bring in to see me, you are increasing my risk of losing my best employees if word that I am seeking a buyer should get out.

I am tired of your cavalier attitude toward the suitability of the potential buyers you bring in here. You seem to thing I have nothing better to do with my time than conduct pointless interviews. Frankly, considering the enormous fees you charge and my questionable return on investment, I think I'm entitled to be angry and frustrated, and I am.

Steve, I have been running this company for 30

years. Perhaps you can imagine my feeling for an enterprise in which I've invested so much time and energy. It's incredibly hard for me even to contemplate turning it over to anyone else, unless one of my children is interested, which seems unlikely. But I feel especially betrayed by your dragging in as prospective buyers people who are utterly unqualified. It's not appropriate, and it's not fair. Just wanted you to know how I feel.

Sincerely,

Well, he makes it clear how he feels, all right. Look at the emotionally charged language he uses: *entitled, angry and frustrated, betrayed, not fair.* Words like these, especially piled up as they are, have little or no place in business writing. He's also dragged in a lot of irrelevant material: a walk-through of what his job entails, the demands on his time, his children's lack of interest in the business.

If you can't write objectively because you're angry or feeling ill-used, it's probably better to wait awhile and gain some perspective. Or type the furious letter and close the document until you're calm. Then delete it. Here's the second letter:

Dear Steve:

I enjoyed chatting with Jack Smith yesterday. It seems clear, however, that his work as a technician and his lack of financial assets qualify him poorly to purchase Wyziwhiz Works. The same is true of the last three prospects I have met through you.

Wyziwhiz Works has increased sales by over 23 percent in the past four months, so I am very busy. I am also deeply concerned that word of my intent to sell the company may leak out: you'll recall that two years ago a prospective buyer discussed my plans with an employee, and as a direct result both my sales vice president and my general manager left me for more secure positions.

Bearing these facts in mind, as well as the considerable amount I've invested in your brokerage operation, I ask that you screen prospects most carefully in the future. I appreciate your attention to this matter.

Sincerely,

This writer basically has a grip. Rather than calling attention to his feelings, he cites facts to reinforce his points. He sticks to the subject. As a bonus, this letter is half the length of the first. Which would you rather receive? Don't boycott gripes altogether: a tone of healthy anger may well be justified. I just want to point out that the primary reward for complaining at length is hostility.

☞ **If you must be funny, be very, very careful.** I *hate* having to write those words: there's too little humor in the world as it is, particularly the black and white world of business—but I have to warn you to watch out. A writing teacher of mine once said, where business writing is concerned, "Humor doesn't travel well." Sadly, I have to agree. My suggestion is to limit your repartee to face-to-face or telephone encounters. Why? For two major reasons.

First, your humor may not be taken as it was intended. In most cases, the people you're writing aren't close friends. They may misunderstand, take offense, even be hurt. And with writing you don't get a second chance. If in a conversation your witty remark is greeted with aggrieved or affronted silence, you have an opportunity to redeem yourself: you can explain what you meant, or apologize, or offer to send an attractive gift. With writing, you don't have that luxury. The words sit there on the page, continuing to reverberate, documenting for all time your failure to amuse.

Well, maybe it isn't usually that bad. But it is risky.

Second, your piece may be read by someone other than the person for whom you originally wrote it. You run the risk of appearing obscure or bizarre to this secondary audience. This applies to the copy in the file also. Think about whether you want your clever sallies to surface five years from now and be read by uncomprehending, unappreciative strangers. And it applies to e-mail in spades.

Remember that e-mail isn't private. Modern technology makes it very possible for an unintended recipient to read your messages (see Chapter 4 for more about this). Even without senior management hacking into your e-mail correspondence and failing to chuckle, think very hard about whether you'd be comfortable if someone copied your e-mail witticisms to your group or a wider audience. People can be surprisingly thoughtless about doing so, so be careful.

Yes, once in a great while someone goes for the jocular vein in print and gets away with it. My friend Arthur runs a summer program for elementary school children. His direct-mail campaign each spring consists of one letter, which begins with a cheery salutation along the lines of *"Helloooo, fellow campers! George of the Jungle here!"* (Body English Arthur's.) People who aren't familiar with Arthur are mystified or scared. Luckily, Arthur's program is so terrific it doesn't matter: the moms who know are careful to clue in those who don't. So Arthur doesn't really care what people think of his letters, or his sense of humor. He just goes on expressing himself. But that's a luxury most of us can't afford.

In conclusion, be attentive to these seven issues of tone, even if you don't happen to be feeling all the right feelings toward your audience. As Lady Macbeth was fond of telling her spouse, "Assume a virtue if you have it not." You'll convince readers that you are kind, trustworthy, sensitive, and on their side—combining, in fact, the best features of the Boy Scouts and I'm OK You're OK therapy.

—— THE BOTTOM LINE ——

- **Write positively, not negatively.**

- **Write surely, not tentatively.**

- **Don't manipulate your readers, at least not overtly.**

- **Remove stiff or dated language.**

- **Apologize immediately and completely.**

- **Don't whine on and on about someone's mistake.**

- **Handle humor cautiously, if at all.**

CHAPTER 4

HAVE I RESPECTED THE BUSINESS E-MAIL DIFFERENCE?

Because it's so quickly become essential for business communication today, I'm giving e-mail its own chapter. The Internet has changed the world, in many ways for the better. I suspect there are few people in the country today who don't have e-mail access, either at home or at work, or both. What a wonderful way to get a message to a friend, instantly, without intruding on either person's schedule! Or to send a copy of a recipe, poem, or photograph. (My husband says if the telephone had somehow been invented *after* the Internet, we'd all be raving about this fabulous new invention, the phone—but my husband is an electronic Luddite, like the nutty guys who destroyed textile machinery in early 19th century England, and refuses even to look at a computer screen. You have to print out anything you want him to see.)

I'm talking about correspondence with family and friends, but I'm sure you also communicate online at work. A lot. It's almost always much easier to write a note, schedule a meeting, send a memo around, or share copy over the Internet, than to accomplish these same tasks by phone, fax, or letter. In fact, e-mail has revolutionized the workplace, and most of us are grateful.

At the same time I want to offer some grumblings and warnings. There is an enormous difference between the e-mail you send to a friend and the e-mail you send to a coworker or senior management. Some people, particularly young people, haven't learned this distinction. My specific concerns about using e-mail in a business context are fourfold. If you bear them in mind, e-mail is a tool almost beyond price. If you don't, you could get into trouble.

1. **A few things shouldn't be written via e-mail, period.** Let's get this category out of the way first:

   Don't e-mail news of a personal nature, especially painful news. I don't really think you'd do this, but it has happened. Some people want to distance themselves from the emotional impact of news such as this: Something happened to your child in day care. Your wife has been taken to the hospital. Your dog was hit by a car. If you should be the one to break the news, break it as gently as you can, in person, and if possible in private.

   Don't send condolences electronically. Write a nice note and put a stamp on it.

   Don't fire anybody by e-mail. You owe the person the human touch here, whatever his or her shortcomings.

2. **Don't be casual.** Why not? It's a casual world. We wear casual dress, we call the boss by his or her first name, we eat with our feet ... just kidding. But because when you write, you document, your business writing needs to be scrupulously correct—e-mail included. I'm not trying to take the fun out of online messaging, but I am forcefully urging you to err on the side of caution. Your e-mail may be forwarded to a third party, maybe even the boss—let's call him Barclay, since we're on a first-name basis. Would you want Barclay to see the following message?

> rob—heads up, meeting at 3 (asuming I can stay awake that long). Don't be late, it's gonna be great. big beth has some ideas that are rockin. Till 3, me ☺

Probably not. This kind of writing can make you seem not only less serious about your work, but less committed. The writer certainly doesn't come across as caring much about the job.

It's incredibly important not to be perceived that way. So I'm going to suggest that, insofar as possible, you write as correctly as you're able. I'm talking about business communication here, not chatting online with your friends: when IMing them or whatever, stream-of-semi-consciousness prose is fine. The cutesy abbreviations (ROFL, IMO) are fine. Even those horrible emoticons are fine.

When you're at work, however, forget all that. Write

to the standards in this book. Don't assume a silly or
frivolous tone: play it straight. Write as correctly as
if you were sending a memo to the CEO of your
organization (or someone else's). Think of your e-
mail as a letter, which in most ways it is—it can be
viewed again and again by any number of people, *and*
it documents both your content and your style. So
check your spelling. Don't yield to the temptation of
dropping capital letters and punctuation. I know, I
know—many people do this at work. But you're not
just anybody: you're on the fast track, and you'll do
yourself much more good than harm by writing e-
mail properly.

I said properly, not pompously. Write in a conversational style: you should be able to read your e-mail
aloud without wincing.

3. **Stop and think before pressing the 'send' button.**
   E-mail makes it easy—far too easy—to send a message or reply at almost the speed of sound. If you're
   angry about something, and if you have a snappy
   trigger finger, it's tempting to rip off a message that
   will only add to the damage. Slow down. Reflect on
   how easy it will be to send this e-mail. Then reflect
   that it's just as easy for someone else to hit a button
   and send it round the whole department. Please, for
   your recipient(s) and for yourself, give it a little time.
   Whether you've written in righteous indignation or
   a nasty fit of temper, stop. Let the e-mail sit for a bit;
   come back to it when you've calmed down; see

whether you really want to send it. Could it be worded more diplomatically? Could it hurt someone relatively innocent? Could it be deleted?

You've probably been warned about the hazards of forgetting that your e-mail is *about* a person, and inadvertently sending it *to* the person. This can happen, for example, if you've addressed the e-mail to a group and forgotten that the person you're talking about is part of that group. Stories circulate about this clumsy maneuver that could freeze your blood, up to and including firings. Stop and think about what you're doing: double-check your address box, and for a group, check from one to end of the box to the other before you send.

Another great idea would be not even to write e-mails you wouldn't want someone to read. See the following section.

4. Don't think for a minute that e-mail is private. You probably already know this also. If your company wants to read your e-mail, it has the technology to do so. Even deleted material, if your company has an able IT person, can be reclaimed. So don't write anything you wouldn't want senior management to read. The message to Rob, above, would certainly qualify in this category. So would anything derogatory about coworkers or clients.

Remember, too, that if someone wants to add a comment on your original message and forward it around the department, they may not reread to see whether remarks contained in your message could backfire. I suspect carelessness, not malice, is at the root of this behavior, but plenty of damage can be done anyway. Take preventive action: write as if everybody's looking.

A final note: considering that it isn't private, it's risky to e-mail your friends on company time. That's why Al Gore invented the lunch hour. And *never* share sensitive information about the company with outsiders.

⸻ THE BOTTOM LINE ⸻

- **Remember that business e-mail is different from e-mail between friends.**

- **Remember that e-mailing isn't always appropriate.**

- **Write as straightforwardly and correctly as if you were writing a conventional letter to someone important.**

- **Think hard before sending.**

- **Never write anything in an e-mail that you wouldn't want others to see.**

CHAPTER 5

HAVE I PREFERRED ACTIVE TO PASSIVE VERBS?

Your boss may return a piece of writing to you for revision with comments such as "You need to zero in on the concept—tighten it up" or "It seems sort of unclear—kind of wordy, too." That's frustrating for you: however, remember it's frustrating for your boss as well. While I can't say for sure what you may be doing wrong, it's a good guess that part of your problem is an overreliance on passive verb constructions. And though people often can't put their finger on just what's the matter with writing that's passive intensive, they know they don't like it.

If you've never thought about the difference between active and passive verb forms, it's time you did. The active, or *to do*, form of a verb is simply a past, present, or future verb, usually paired with a subject, and looking more or less like these examples:

I led   we *have accomplished*
He says   you *will send*

A passive, or *to be done*, verb form is the past tense of a verb—
led, accomplished, said, sent—with any form of the verb *to be*:

> I *was led*   the job *was accomplished*
> it *will be said*   the letter *has been sent*

I will get out on my customary limb and say that the passive
is an inferior, clumsy verb form. Nine times out of ten you don't
need it and shouldn't use it. Having said so, I'll take three minutes to show you three uses for it. If you can't show you're using
the passive voice for one of these three reasons, you should cut
it from your piece without mercy.

☞ **Use the passive voice in three situations.** I won't deny
it: passive verbs can be useful. You can use them

1. When you don't know who did something:

   The gun *was fired* at close range.

2. To protect a person or organization:

   A mistake was made in Customer Service. On behalf
   of Astro, I apologize for any inconvenience our error
   has caused.

(It was Betsy's first day on the job: let's give her another chance. If this customer gets her name, she's toast.)

3. Occasionally, if the object of your sentence is much more the news or the point:

> President Reagan *was shot* on his way to the Capitol steps.

> The final draft *was collated, addressed, and mailed* in less than four hours.

Readers may care considerably less who shot: the president is the focus of attention. And they may not care at all, depending on the context, what exhausted persons collated, addressed, and mailed. In fact, if different persons performed the operations, the sentence would become impossibly unwieldy:

> In less than four hours, Michele collated the final draft, Duane addressed the envelopes, and Jason took all the copies to the mailbox.

The only possible justification for such writing is that you are showcasing the stars of your organization and how hard they work. *Do not* take Rule 3 as

---

a license to start using the passive voice indiscriminately. *Do not* overwork the form. *The passive voice can run you into trouble if you use it as a default mode on ordinary occasions.*

☞ **Prefer the active mode in virtually every other situation.** Overuse of the passive voice is an unwholesome habit. What's wrong with it? A couple of things.

> It *was decided* to shift the report deadline to April 2.
> John *was expected* to present the report today.
> The PC *was removed* last week.

It's a strength of this voice that, in these examples as in those preceding, it allows you to omit the initiator of the action from the sentence. Yet, paradoxically, it can also be a serious weakness. Dropping the prime mover and shaker from your sentence **can make you look bad**: evasive, shifty, possibly trying to avoid blame.

> Your tax records *seem to have been mislaid.*

Or timid, or poorly informed, or vague, or stupid. Hm. I'm beginning to wonder whether it's worth it.

And that's not all. If you do include the perpetrator, it **always takes more words** to write in the passive:

Active: The accountant *cooked* the books.

Passive: The books *were cooked* by the
          accountant.

Why take up space with needless words? And these are those words.

Last, the passive voice **inverts and subverts action**. Since written English runs from left to right, the action of a sentence typically takes the same route. In an archetypal active sentence, a *subject* does an *action* to an *object*. For example:

The accountant *cooked* the books.

The structure of a passive sentence, however, runs counter to expectation, i.e., from right to left.

The books *were cooked* by the accountant.

All right, so it's not exactly flying in the face of nature. But it's a little odd. And the inversion can make the writing seem static, action-poor.

Give yourself points for every unnecessary passive verb you

rewrite in the active voice. If you're being honest, you'll see that few of them are really justified:

> Passive: The minutes *were read* by the secretary.

> Active: The secretary *read* the minutes.

You may have to do some work if you've used a passive verb to hide the fact that you don't know something you should:

> Passive: The prize *will be presented* at tomorrow's department meeting.
> (If you have no idea who's handing it out, it's definitely time to inquire.)

> Active: President and CEO John Allen will present the prize at…
> (Incontestably a better line overall.)

Sometimes you can simply choose a different verb:

> Passive: Passengers *were awarded* 500 bonus miles for the flight.

> Active: Passengers *received* 500 bonus miles for the flight.

To help you spot passive verbs, look for *to be* in any of its forms—*will have been* seen, *was* expected, *was to have been* given. It can be a clue that passives have crept into your writing, generally to its disadvantage.

——THE BOTTOM LINE——

- **Choose passive verbs only if**
  - **the doer of the action is unknown**
  - **you want to protect the doer**
  - **the object of action is the point, rather than the doer**
- **Remember that passive verbs can**
  - **make you look shifty or evasive**
  - **make your sentence wordy**
  - **cause the action of the sentence to run in reverse**

CHAPTER 6

HAVE I USED THE RIGHT WORD?

Choosing and using words correctly will raise your score with your boss and your readers. It's a pleasure when a writer drops in the *mot juste*, or just-right word (well, maybe not your idea of pleasure, but discriminating readers enjoy it, and we aim to please). Unfortunately, by the same token, use of the wrong word will significantly undermine the confidence of a fastidious reader, which no one can afford to do. And your spell checker blithely passes on the misuse of words. Here are assorted pairs and snares that can trip business writers, causing them to convey an unintended image to their readers—an unfortunate subtext that makes them appear to be in poor control of their material. (Would you buy a vowel from this person?)

I have listed below four categories of words that cause trouble: confused, misused, abused, and not to be used. Please pay close attention if people have accused you of malapropisms (after Mrs. Malaprop, the Sheridan heroine guilty of committing "putrefied with fear" and other linguistic enormities) or if you yourself suspect your word choices are sometimes a few degrees off.

☞ **Confused.** In this category are words that look or sound alike. In business writing, the most familiar pairs include the following. If you don't want to have to keep referring to the list, I've added some memory boosters you may find helpful.

averse	adj. against or unwilling: " I am *averse* to the idea of a merger."
adverse	adj. unfavorable: "Don't risk an *adverse* credit rating."

affect	v: to have an impact on; n: capacity for emotional response
effect	v: to bring about: "*effect* a change"; n: result: "the *effect* of the restructuring"

Remember: the two most useful senses of each word are alphabetical. First, you *affect* something or someone; then you see the *effect*. *Affect* as a noun is unlikely to be part of business writing. As for *effect* as a verb, you're on your own.

any time	whenever: *any time* you're feeling blue
anytime	at any time whatsoever: call us *anytime*, day or night

capital	available cash; town or city that is seat of government
capitol	the building where state legislature meets
Capitol	Washington, D.C., building where U.S. Congress meets

compare to	to suggest a similarity: "He compared me *to* James Reston."
compare with	to make an examination of two things, addressing their differences and similarities: "We compared the figures *with* those of the preceding quarter."

Remember: in business writing, you're almost always comparing *with*. Comparing *to* is more frequent in literature: "Shall I compare thee to a summer's day?"

complement	to form a valuable part of, to add to in a positive way
compliment	to praise or pay a compliment to

Remember: *Complement* is probably the word you want; it's generally the more useful in a business context. To me, the first five letters of the word look like the word "couple," which is what complementing is—a productive joining of two parts.

continual	again and again: "*continual* objections from the Senate floor"
continuous	uninterrupted: "a *continuous* flow of new business"

Remember: The last three letters of continu*ous* stand for "one uninterrupted sequence." (I really wish I'd thought that up.)

council	governing body
counsel	lawyer, advice; to advise
ensure	to guarantee
insure	to cover by selling or purchasing insurance

Remember: *in*sure with *in*surance. Although most dictionaries allow you to use *insure* for both meanings, this distinction is one many insurance companies themselves prefer to make. You won't offend anyone by making it, but you might offend someone if you don't.

farther	a greater distance
further	in greater depth, more

Remember: *far*ther refers to *a*ctual distance. *The American Heritage Dictionary* notes that these words have been used interchangeably until recently, and its Usage Panel (for more about this group, see Chapter 12) says "the distinction is not always easy to draw." Just be aware that it exists in many people's minds.

flounder	to struggle, thrash about in confusion
founder	to fail utterly, sink to the bottom

Remember: The *l* in f*l*ounder stands for life, and while there's life there's hope. For a *foundering* enterprise, there is no hope. It has collapsed down to its origins, or *foundations*.

pedal	v. to propel, as a bicycle, by the act of moving pedals
peddle	v. to sell, or attempt to sell

If it weren't for influence peddling, we wouldn't need this in a business writing book. Unfortunately, these two words sound exactly alike, but they don't share any element of meaning. The word you're likely to want is *peddle*, a not-very-complimentary synonym for *sell*.

principal	n. capital as opposed to interest; important person, head of school; adj.: main, primary
principle	n. basic truth, rule, or policy

Remember: Not hard if you bear in mind that *principle* is a noun with just one meaning: a basic truth, tenet, etc. Everything else, noun or adjective, is *principal*.

saving	a reduction in cost or expense
savings	the plural of saving, with the same meaning

You can realize *a saving* or *savings*, e.g., if you shop at Sam's Club. You cannot realize a *savings*. It's as incorrect as saying *a briefcases* or *a meetings*. It just happens more often. I hadn't paid much attention to the issue until a senior executive noted how deeply she disliked *a savings* in her company's advertising. In fact, she was taking it out of copy and giving the advertising agency a piece of her mind every time she found it. *The American Heritage Dictionary* Usage Panel is with her on this one: 57 percent of the panel found the phrase unacceptable. Says the panel, in one of its many interesting Usage Notes, "*a saving* is the only uncontroversial form."

Think no one will notice if you're a letter or two off? Here's a story just for you. I once got a call the night before Thanksgiving from a friend, an advertising copywriter who seemed oddly insistent that I okay "We'll help compl*i*ment your needs."

"It's sort of like being polite to them, right?" said Kevin. "Paying them a compliment?"

"Of course it isn't," I answered. "Tell me you didn't."

"I did," he admitted. On two thousand brochures. Instead of perfecting his pecan pie recipe, he spent the night gluing two thousand tiny little e's on top of i's because his boss was so furious she refused to pay for a reprint. This didn't have to happen. Make sure it doesn't happen to you.

☞ **Misused.** This category includes pairs that are wrongly thought to be interchangeable. It also includes words that many business writers use incorrectly.

amount	They are different, but it's easy to know which to use.
number	Write *number*, not *amount*, for things you can count. It's therefore "the *number* of pennies," but "the *amount* of cash."

ambiguous	unclear in meaning or intent
ambivalent	uncertain in one's feelings

Again, the alphabet helps out here. First comes the unclear item, which is ambi*g*uous; then follows the reaction, which is ambi*v*alent.

| **among** | amid more than two: "You're *among* friends" |
| **between** | usually said of two things: "A choice *between* two strategies" |

However, consider "talks between Germany, France, and Italy" or "Relations between Jane and her two assistants have never been good." *Among* doesn't sound right in these sentences. Some people suggest that when the action is going between all possible two-somes (Germany and France, Germany and Italy, France and Italy), the proper choice is *between*. Others simply say the distinction is not all that clear. You can let your ear be your guide, or you can rephrase your sentence: "Jane has never gotten along with her two assistants."

| **bring** | to carry (literally or figuratively) toward |
| **take** | to carry (literally or figuratively) away |

I've seen this distinction in almost every manual I've ever read, so somebody must be misusing these words. If it's you, stop it. We're not going to waste any more of our time on it.

| **comprise** | to include |
| **compose** | to make up |

Remember my suggestion that you write defensively? *Comprise* is often used nowadays as a synonym for *compose*, as in "The board is comprised of six members," and it bothers some people. I get to hear about it. (Get into this business and these people will pick on you at parties as though you were responsible.) Although this meaning has now achieved dictionary status, a number of well-educated people prefer the original meaning, roughly synonymous with embrace. Why risk annoying anyone? No one will notice if you *don't* use *comprise* in its nouveau sense. Here's how to please everyone:

> The board *comprises* six members.
> The board *is composed of* representatives from each region.

enormity   In its most precise sense refers to awfulness, rather than size. "The *enormity* of his crime overwhelmed him."

evoke   to call forth
invoke   to call upon

Remember your Latin: the meanings are direct translations. If time and trouble have wiped Latin from your memory, go with *evoke*, which is what we usually try to do with a response. *Invoke* may involve calling on the spirits of ancestors, gods, former employers, thus tending to be a little poetic for business writing. But it is useful when someone calls on a law or principle, such as client-customer privilege.

> The drop in the Dow *evoked* mass selloffs.
> The plaintiff *invoked* the Fifth Amendment.

fewer, less   like *amount* and *number*. If you can't separate and count the items under discussion, write *less*: "*Less* disturbance in the bond market." If you can count them, it's *fewer*: "We hired *fewer* employees than last year."

fulsome   offensively insincere. When you offer fulsome praise, you are not necessarily praising something in the fullest sense, although some dictionaries allow that meaning. Fulsome has the unique meaning of praising hypocritically: with fulsome praise, you are overdoing it (in fact, you are full of it).

i.e.   that is, in other words. From Latin *id est*
e.g.   for example. From Latin *exempli gratia*
(Note that these familiar little abbreviations are not usually italicized.)

imply   to suggest without openly stating
infer   to gather from something said or written

These are easy to distinguish, although too many people don't. The chronology is alphabetical: you have to imply something before anything can be inferred.

individual   Avoid using this word as a synonym for *person*: "I've asked two *individuals* to handle this project." Use it as a noun only if you are distinguishing a person from a group: "One *individual* stands out in this department."

lay   to put or place; past is *laid*
lie   to recline; for inanimate objects, to be in a horizontal
     position; past is *lay*

Let's *lay* this error to rest. I will no longer take it *lying* down.

like   Don't use *like* as a synonym for *as if, such as*, or *as*. If
     you've written a *like* you don't like, try substituting each
     of the three:

     He looks *like* he needs a break. (Only *as if* works.)
     We need a motto, *like* "Excelsior." (*Such as* makes
     sense, sounds good.)
     He is a hard worker, *like* you said. (It should be *as*.)

Some people have trouble differentiating between *like* and *as* in a sentence such as that last one. You should find it easy if you remember that *like* precedes a noun and *as* precedes a verb:

     If it walks *like* a duck, quacks *like* a duck...
     Just *as* I said, just *as* I am...

literally in a literal, or by-the-book, sense: really and truly
figuratively in a metaphorical sense; *not* really or truly

For heaven's sake, don't misuse these. Your reader will think you are a figurative dodo. Even in conversation, you crash and burn with a line such as "I was literally dead on my feet." Your listeners will be looking for signs of necrosis. Get a grip: you were *figuratively* dead. Employing *literally* as an all-purpose intensifier suggests that you think the almost-right word will do. Or that you are clueless.

may	refers to future activity in a present-tense context
might	refers to future activity in a past-tense context

> He says he *may* join Arnold Advisory Services.
> He said he *might* join Arnold Advisory Services.

It's as simple as that—with, this being English, the usual additional quirk: to indicate a significant shade of doubt, use *might* in the present context: "He *might* join us, although his train doesn't get in until 5:00 and we're meeting at 5:15."

noisome	means obnoxious, odorous, or toxic; not a synonym for *noisy*
select	adj. special, exclusive: "a *select* group of investors"
selected	adj. chosen from a group: "*selected* items are on sale"

There's an overlap of meaning—both adjectives imply a process of selection—but only in the first case is superiority the criterion for being chosen. We may or may not know why the *selected* items were selected.

shall, will   Why bother with *shall*, when you can use *will?* At best, you're dealing with a verb form that's increasingly rare; at worst, you'll come across as affected. Leave *shall* to the writers of contracts.

that   used without a comma to introduce a defining clause
which   preceded by a comma, used to introduce a descriptive clause

In his classic, *Modern English Usage*, H. W. Fowler took *seven* pages to explain this; quite a few contemporary manuals shed similar amounts of ink over it. So you can read about it in tremendous detail elsewhere if you wish. The issue is whether one says "the book *that* I gave you" or "the book, *which* I gave you." The short answer is that if you precede the word with a comma, it should be *which*. Otherwise you should use *that*. For example:

> *Winning, which* I gave you for your birthday, is Jack Welch's second book.

> The book *that* I gave you last week is out of print.

The long answer: *which* introduces a descriptive clause. Such a clause adds information that may be helpful but that could be omitted. *That* introduces restrictive, crucial information that cannot be omitted from the sentence. The first sentence, above, without the *which* clause, stands alone: the information in the clause—"which I gave you for your birthday"—is interesting and important but not necessary to the integrity of the sentence. We indicate this by using a comma or pair of commas. Without the *that* clause, on the other hand, the second sentence is meaningless. "The book is out of print"? *What* book is out of print? The *that* clause is crucial to identifying the book. We emphasize the essential nature of such a clause by omitting a comma and using *that.*

A smart friend of mine notes that in business writing, *that* is probably the word we should be using most of the time. Her point is that we don't need any "by-the-way" additions. Information-intensive writing deals with crucial facts we can't omit. Her assertion puts her in good company: experts estimate that nine times out of ten, *that* will be correct. So try it first, and if it works, keep it.

☞ **Abused.** Another way of putting it is **overused**. This category includes words that have been put together according to standard English principles, with results that have become faddish. In each case, the word given stands for a raft of similar ones.

impact, to   The recently updated *Fowler's Modern English Usage* was taken to task by some critics when it appeared for approving this use of *impact*. Note, however, that a cartoon in the *Wall Street Journal* considerably longer ago showed a manager telling his subordinate, "As I men-

tioned before, Fassler, you'll never go anywhere until you
start using 'impact' as a verb." Whatever. I'd be careful
not to overexpose this and other noun-to-verb constructions. *Affect* is, by the way, a fine synonym for *impact*.

English is enormously flexible. One facet of its flexibility is
the ability to take one part of speech and turn it into another,
thus effectively creating a new word. Many words so created
have become respectable residents of the dictionary. The practice adds to the texture and charm of English. I would advise,
however, not overdoing the creativity thing by recklessly turning words into verbs, or as Calvin of the much-missed comic
strip "Calvin and Hobbes" puts it, "verbing." As Calvin notes,
"Verbing weirds language." How true, as the next example
demonstrates.

incentivize   Good grief. We have a perfectly nice word for this concept: *motivate*. Why do we need *incentivize*, which is truly
hideous? The original word was a noun, *incentive*, that
got verbed—an egregious example of "izification," illustrating another strength of our language that all too
easily becomes a liability.

Again in accordance with the rich traditions of English,
which borrows liberally from every language it meets, our
mother tongue happily incorporated the Romans' practice of
adding suffixes to form new words. The result is such shockers
as *incentivize*. As if prioritize and demilitarize weren't enough.
Because these and many other "-izes" are included in most dic-

tionary in good standing, I can't forbid you to use them. But I do cordially counsel restraint. Limit yourself to one or two per communication, and for goodness' sake, don't start making up your own. There is no rational excuse for *Fidelityize* or *videoize*.

enthuse   More verbing. This back formation from *enthusiasm* pains a majority of the *American Heritage*'s Usage Panel. I'd avoid it.

intuit   Still more verbing. This one's been around for a long time, but, again, the Usage Panel dislikes it—and they're not alone. Another one to avoid.

-wise   As in public education-wise An infelicitous use of a principle similar to that which generates the *-izes*, above, though *-wise* typically creates temporary words—usually not great ones. My clever friend Connie, a writer, and other authorities on style feel that it should be avoided at all costs. I agree. At least don't use it if you can come up with something better. For example, which sentence is more appealing?

Consumers have become more *careful dollar-wise*.

Consumers are spending more carefully.

By comparison with the second sentence, the first seems lazy and imprecise. All right for a first draft, but not for final copy.

☞ **Not to be used.** This category includes words that are not in the dictionary or are listed in it as "nonstandard." To me that's kiss-of-death time. Some are jargon, some are colloquial or dialect, some are simply errors. Unless you are certain you're writing to readers who share and appreciate your vocabulary, don't lead the dictionary. Eventually, if a word is derivatively sound and useful, it will find its way to a respectable listing in *American Heritage* or *Webster's*. Until then, don't use it. The list includes, but is by no means limited to, the following:

> alot
> alright
> anyways
> heighth
> incent
> irregardless
> nother, as in "a whole *nother*"
> regards, as in "in *regards* to"

——— THE BOTTOM LINE ———

- Don't confuse, misuse, or abuse words.

- Don't use words that are substandard or nonexistent.

- Use this guide or your dictionary if you aren't sure.

CHAPTER 7

DO I HAVE TOO MANY WORDS?

Too many words make for a fine first draft—easy and quick to write. A famous line, which I've heard attributed to everyone from Herodotus to Emerson to Ross Perot (What a crew!) is, "If I had had more time, I would have written you a shorter letter." Blaise Pascal said it first, or at least the gist of it. He wrote in 1657: "I've made this letter longer than usual, only because I didn't have time to make it shorter." Yes, it's tedious, time-consuming work to make something long shorter. To a great extent, that's how editors make a living, and that's why they get paid for it.

This doesn't mean you should try to limit your verbiage in your initial draft. Cut loose with that first fine careless rapture; get it down on paper, however windy and profligate you are with the words. Then get rid of the extra ones. That, of course, is where the art lies. You could say of good writing what Michelangelo said about sculpting: you just remove everything that isn't part of the statue. He also called sculpting "an art that takes away superfluous materials." That's exactly what you want to do. Sounds easy. You know it isn't, either in constructing a great sculpture or creating a good piece of writing. Here are some strategies for chiseling away nonessential sentence elements.

☞ **Eliminate roundabout phrases.** The media constantly set a bad example by using such phrases as "a precipitation event" and "an accident scene." Even if they can't bring themselves to say that it's raining or somebody smashed up a car, why do they have to add the words "event" and "scene"? Take them out: do you miss them? Resist such phrases when you write: the media's bad behavior is no excuse for yours.

You add nothing but mass to your piece with the following phrases. They are rarely justified: note how easily you can edit them out—in itself a clue:

the field of	the sum of
the study of	it is
the fact is that	there is, there are

The field of science is a fascinating one.

Science is fascinating.

It is easy to see *that* the production department is understaffed.

The production department is clearly understaffed.

The fact is that it is as difficult *as it is* important to keep tight control of receivables.

Keeping tight control of receivables is important
but difficult.

There are four keys *that* control movement for this
program.

Four keys control movement for this program.

Here are a few others and their space-saving equivalents:

it would be appreciated if	please
would you be so kind as to	please
in the approximate area of	about
in the majority of instances	usually
in the not-too-distant future	soon
at this point in time	at this time, now

Watch for these and similar phrases. Why add stuff without
substance?

☞ **Don't pile on pairs of negatives.** Writing with double
negatives—"not unusual" for "usual"—is a stylistic tic dating back
at least to the 18th century, when the phenomenon was discovered
by Bishop Robert Loth. (I didn't make it up. Grammar people live
for this kind of thing.) Anyway, double negatives verge on cute,
and they take up room: they're out of place in business writing
unless you're conveying a particularly fine shade of meaning.

Often the meaning of a sentence is unchanged when you strike out pairs of negatives such as these:

> We should *avoid prohibiting* people who are *not uncommitted* to the project from attending.

> We should let people who are committed to the project attend.

> Bruce was *not unfair* to his employees, and they expressed their *not insincere* appreciation.

> Bruce was fair to his employees, and they expressed their sincere appreciation.

☞ **Edit out "prepositional phrase freight."** In business writing, we're usually trying to impart information. As a result, we're often tempted to try to convey just one more fact or suggestion, jam one more bit of helpful data, into a sentence. The writing becomes heavy and overloaded. Remember the five Ws of journalism—who, what, where, when, and why? As I recall, you're supposed to incorporate all five into a lead megasentence for your article or press release. Unfortunately, it rarely works. Fitting that much information into one sentence typically results in an overweight construction:

> The leaders of the nations of the Pacific Rim will meet at a conference in a suburb of Seoul on June

19, 2007, to seek ways to cut the cost of durable
goods that are intended for distribution to
countries in the western hemisphere.

Oh, dear. What we have here is a series of prepositional
phrases strung together. You can recognize them by their form,
which is consistent: a small word, often one of location—*at, by,
up, over, under, for, with*—and its object. The prepositional phrases in the sentence above are

of the nations	on June 19, 1999
of the Pacific Rim	of durable goods
at a conference	for distribution
in a suburb	to countries
of Seoul	in the western hemisphere

You can see that most of the sentence is prepositional phrase
freight, and its weight has deep-sixed the sentence. You can do
a lot to shrink or eliminate these phrases. Perhaps most easily,
you can turn them into adjectives: the phrase "of the nations"
can become "nation," "of Seoul" can become "Seoul"—or verbs:
(meet) "at a conference" can be transformed into "confer."

Another smart move is to divide the data between two sentences.

Leaders of the Pacific Rim nations will confer June
19, 2007, in a Seoul suburb. They will seek ways to
cut the cost of durable goods distributed to
countries in the Western Hemisphere.

Be wary, however, of going too far along this route. Jack the Ripper editing—ripping and chopping—is an activity to avoid. If you shrink and squeeze those prepositional phrases too far, your prose eventually becomes all but impenetrable. The result is something that newsman Jack Hart engagingly refers to as "densepack" and I call the Black Hole School of Writing:

> Pacific Rim nation leaders confer in a Seoul suburb
> June 19, 2007, on cost-cutting measures targeted
> at Western Hemisphere durable goods distribution.

And what we have *here* is a failure to communicate. The new sentence is a sort of shorthand for the original, with something definitely lost in translation. In fact, it's practically impossible to translate. You can edit more gently and still keep to a reasonable length. With a reasonable hope of being understood.

Note that prepositional phrases don't always indicate a load of information. They may simply be the sign of a first draft, loosely put together. Tighten it up on your next pass:

> Loose: On Monday, September 2, the CEO of
>   this company will give a presentation
>   with slides to those of us in the areas of
>   marketing and sales.

> Edited: Our company CEO will give a slide
>   presentation Monday, September 2, to
>   our marketing and sales areas.

☞ **Keep the action in your verbs.** Look at the following verb forms. They're wordy and they're ineffective—an unpleasant combination:

> to have a tendency
> to be a participant
> to do an analysis
> to show a preference
> to give a demonstration

What's gone wrong? Glad you asked. The verbs that should be the driving force or propulsion of the sentence have gone into hiding and reemerged as *nouns: preference, analysis.* Note that's where the action, such as it is, exists, not in the weak, action-poor verbs *to have, to be,* and so forth. As a result, the phrases are not only wordy, they are static, stripped of vigor. Here are the "real" verbs, restored to their proper places:

> to tend
> to participate
> to analyze
> to prefer
> to demonstrate

Shorter, stronger, and more interesting. Short little helping verbs, such as *to do* or *to be,* can alert you to this flaw in your own writing.

Edit for all these indiscretions before you print your final draft. Be relentless: not even you, let alone anyone else, will miss this stuff when it's gone.

—— THE BOTTOM LINE ——

- Get rid of roundabout constructions.

- Eliminate double negatives.

- Unload prepositional phrase freight.

- Check that the action is in your verbs, not nouns.

CHAPTER 8

HAVE I SPICED MY WRITING WITH VARIETY?

If your boss complains your writing lacks zip, sex appeal, or pizzazz, it may be suffering a surfeit of sameness. In that case, you need to inject some variety. Moderation's a key principle here—because if you use any technique *im*moderately, you're losing variety, not gaining it. Here are a few tips to inject the right level of this important commodity into your writing.

☞ **Vary your paragraphs in length.** Everyone knows a certain amount of white space is a good thing for eye appeal and relief. Some people think you need to bullet out everything to achieve this. At the moment, I think, bulleting suffers from overexposure, and it adds to overall copy length. But the idea is basically a good one.

In fact, you can easily get white space by changing the configuration of your paragraphs. If you have a heavy block of text in which you have discussed three concepts, for instance, break it into three paragraphs, each with a topic sentence. While you're at it, use the topic sentence that applied to all three concepts as a one-sentence paragraph: very catchy. Visually, you'll get a design scheme that looks something like this:

XXXXX XXXXXX XXXXXXX XXXXXXXXX.

XXX XXXXXX XXXX XXX XXXXXXX XXXXXX
XXXX XXXXXXXX XX, XXX XXXX XXXXXXXXXXX
XXXXXXXX XX XXX XXXXX XX XXXXX.

XXXXXXXXX, XXXXXX XXX XXXXX XXXXXXX
XX XXX XXXXXXX XX XXXXXXXX XXXXXXXX
XXXX XXXX; XXXX XX XXXXXXXXXXX XX
XXXXX XXXXXXXX.

XXXX XX XXX XXXX XX XXXX XXXXXXXXXX XX
XXX XXXXXXX XXXX. XX XXX XXXXX XXXX XXX
XXXXXXX XXX XXXXX XXX XXXX.

instead of this:

XXXXX XXXXXX XXXXXXX XXXXXXXXX.
XXX XXXXXX XXXX XXX XXXXXXX XXXXXX
XXXX XXXXXXXX XX, XXX XXXX XXXXXXXXXXX
XXXXXXXX XX XXX XXXXX XX XXXXX.
XXXXXXXXX, XXXXXX XXX XXXXX XXXXXXX
XX XXX XXXXXXX XX XXXXXXXX XXXXXXXX
XXXX XXXX; XXXX XX XXX. XXXX XX XXX
XXXX XX XXXX XXXXXXXXXX XX XXX XXXXXXX
XXXX. XX XXX XXXXX XXXX XXX XXXXXXXXXX
XX XXXXXXX XXX XXXXX XXX XX XXXXX XXXXXXXX.

Depending on your needs for the piece as a whole, this could represent a welcome change. It's also useful if you're dealing with hard or unfamiliar concepts.

☞ **Vary the length of your sentences.** Throw a short sentence in among the longer ones when you think of it. As I've mentioned, business writing is almost by definition expository and information intensive: therefore, a short sentence gives readers a break. Also, particularly if you are dealing with material that's technical, or unfamiliar to your readers, be sure to shorten up sentences overall. A larger number of shorter sentences will be a blessing to them.

> The recent legislation, passed by an overwhelming majority in both houses and signed into law by the president in June, clarifies the tax status of certain types of insurance, allowing tax-favorable treatment similar to that already enjoyed by other forms of health insurance, and as such validates these types of coverage as mainstream insurance products.

Not a thing wrong with the grammar, but a reader who attempts it in one bite may require the Heimlich maneuver. Cut it into small pieces as an aid to digestion.

☞ **Vary sentences in form.** It's unlikely to the vanishing point that readers will notice you're doing this. However, if you don't, your writing may bore them. A string of declarative sentences—*I did this. He did that. The system crashed*—gets old. So does the overuse of any form, for that matter:

> *Barring an unforeseen change* in the money markets, our IPO should be quite successful. *Taking advantage of a lull* in the commodities market, we consider our timing to be unusually opportune. *Remembering our difficulties* in the past, we feel extremely fortunate.

And hoping to hear from you soon, we remain your humble servant. Stylistic tics such as this can not only be annoying but can actually interfere with your concentration. You've got a whole range of ways to assemble thoughts into sentences that look and sound different. Here's a thought from an annual report, expressed in various ways:

> Our residential real estate loan business increased by $200 million as a result of mortgage refinancing.

> Bolstered by mortgage refinancing, our residential real estate loan business increased by $200 million.

> Our residential real estate loan business increased by $200 million. We attribute the rise to mortgage refinancing.
> We refinanced many mortgages, and our residential real estate loan business increased by $200 million.

☞ **Vary word length.** The same principle applies to words. If they aren't varied in length, you are probably in trouble. Too many short words not only look bad, but may be a sign that you haven't moved far enough from a loose, first-draft style. For instance, look at the following string of pearls:

> It is a bit of a reach to be in favor of the rights of the embezzler.

The series of short words looks choppy, feels wordy. On the flip side, look at the Cuisinart effect you get when you overdo long words:

> Hypervigilance ascertaining commodity availability effectually contravenes competitive challenges.

Chains of long words create a barrier: I think it means something like keep an eye on supply to stay even with the competition, but most people won't bother to translate.

One of my students complained, understandably, "You won't let us use long words; now you won't let us use short words. What words *should* we use?" Of course, I want you to use all of your words. In rotation. A mix of long, short, and in-between words is easy on the eye as well as the brain. A series of words all the same length is a signal to rewrite.

☞ **Don't think variety means everything but the kitchen sink.** A note of caution. Throwing every kind of font, point size, and attention-getting format such as caps and bold-face type into your work in the name of variety is not a good idea. Because word processing makes this instantaneous, the appeal can be seductive. From the reader's standpoint, however, it's surprisingly distracting. Or let's just say less is more. Here's what I mean:

> Get a comprehensive COMBINATION of financial services with the **Bank of Virginia Premium Account**. This account lets you combine _deposit_ and _investment_ balances to waive account fees.

Goodness! the level of excitement is well-nigh intolerable. There's something endearingly Victorian about all the body English, so to speak, but you can see the technique emphasizes form over substance. It also looks as if the writer didn't trust the copy to speak for itself. Observe, shudder, abstain.

There you have the do's and don'ts of variety. Check your writing to be sure you haven't hypnotized your readers with sameness or gone font-happy to attract their attention.

—— THE BOTTOM LINE ——

- **Vary paragraph length, sentence length, sentence form, and word length.**

- **Don't overdo variety in font and type.**

CHAPTER 9

WHEN ALL'S SAID AND DONE, HAVE I AVOID- ED CLICHÉS TO THE NTH DEGREE?

Clichés are another dark side of variety that I didn't touch on in the last chapter because I wanted to give them their own—how shall I put it? place in the sun. (I write all my own stuff.) Clichés are phrases that once were sharp, meaningful, clever. Over time they have lost their luster. Worse, they have almost lost their meaning. Let me elaborate. Take the cliché "My heart skipped a beat," for example. When people first began using it, the metaphor referred to an experience that is truly dramatic. If it's ever happened to you, you know what I mean. Your body shudders at the impact of the arrhythmia produced under the stress of a powerful, emotional moment. Originally the phrase was used to authenticate the intensity of such a moment—the moment when a child stepped out in front of a moving vehicle or a message arrived saying All is lost, or even All is OK. People who had felt heart arrhythmia could relate to this; people who hadn't were awed as well. Alas for the effectiveness of the phrase today—it's been so overused and has lost so much altitude that it now has almost no emotive impact. Someone is likely to say "My heart skipped a beat when I thought I might miss lunch."

Variety is the spice of life. All the world's a stage. Through a glass darkly. It's as plain as the nose on your face. To be or not to be? She's the cream of the crop. When they were new, these phrases engaged heart and senses. The first person who told someone else to have a nice day probably got major credit for charm and thoughtfulness. Nowadays people respond that they've made other plans. The other day I saw a bus I hoped to take. Straining to see the destination in the display slot above the windshield, I read "Have a Nice Day." Not very helpful. In fact, terminally annoying. (I think that's a pun. I get credit, even though it was accidental.)

But what are you going to do? How are you, have a nice day, please don't hesitate to call, all are coin of the realm—you should pardon the expression—in conversation and writing. They move the action along smoothly, if not interestingly. This is a point I appreciate. I'm requesting just three things:

☞ **Keep the numbers down.** Don't string clichés together. You can create a series of them like lily pads on a pond, and leapfrog from one to another without ever coming up with one original thought:

> No: Last but not least, please rest assured that our group stands ready to do everything in our power to ensure that a good time is had by all.

Yes: Finally, we'd like to assure you our group
      will do everything we can to ensure a won-
      derful evening for the Emerald Shillelagh
      Reunion.

☞ **Be sure the cliché is appropriate.** Sentences such as the
following are unsuitable in a business context:

My better half and I look forward to filling the cup
with you and your bride on Saturday.

You asked why our sales went through the roof in
May. Not to beat about the bush, it sure beats the
heck out of me, chief.

Save the arch and the poetic, the catch phrase and the refer-
ential dialogue for your friends, if you must. (Actually, if you
write like this, you may not have any. A lot of people don't
appreciate this stuff from their friends either.)

My wife and I look forward to dinner with you and
Mrs. Archer on Saturday.

You asked why sales increased in May. Candidly
speaking, I have no ready answer.

☞ **Reword clichés when you can.** Your writing will be fresher and more memorable. As you can see from the fixes above, it's not even hard. It just means you have to go off autopilot and think about what you're saying. Now that your consciousness has been raised, it should be easy to recognize *welcome aboard, look before we leap, put a game plan in place*, etc., for the tired, stale material it is. You can do better, and you should.

——— THE BOTTOM LINE ———

- Watch the clichés you use: keep the numbers down.

- Be sure a cliché is business-appropriate.

- Reword clichés if possible.

CHAPTER 10

HAVE I CREATED UNINTENTIONAL "NOISE"?

This chapter is short, but that doesn't mean it's not important. Especially if you're in a hurry or just writing carelessly, you can produce unintentional sound effects, which I call noise. Such tunes and rhythms are unwanted additions to your writing because they distract readers from your points. Needless to say, you can also come across as less than serious or committed in your intent. The charms of frivolity are pretty much lost on captains of industry (see "If you must be funny," in Chapter 3). Your boss is probably no exception, so watch out for noise.

Noise can be easily edited out by reading copy aloud. You can also read it to yourself—I read all my own writing and everyone else's "aloud to myself"—because actually you're editing for noise your readers may hear when reading to *them*selves. (I'm assuming they won't be reading your work aloud, but that could happen as well—maybe in a meeting, where you'd be horribly embarrassed if you'd unintentionally written in iambic pentameter. If you did it intentionally, you have a career problem, or you will soon [See "captains of industry" above]). Here are three areas to monitor:

☞ **Achieving accidental alliteration.** I 'm kidding. But that's a fair example. Alliteration, a string of words with the same first letter, creates terrific poetry and tongue twisters—two things you absolutely don't want in your writing:

> Sarah will sit in on the secretaries' session of the seminar Saturday.

Read the words to yourself and you'll see the unpleasant effect of the repeated sibilant *s*: a delivery irksome enough to obscure the message. Edit for the repetition. (No fair changing Sarah's name or the day of the session.) If they don't immediately spring to mind, you can look up replacements with your Thesaurus command for at least every other offending word. Here's one tolerable rewrite:

> Sarah plans to attend the secretaries' portion of the conference on Saturday.

The fix isn't hard. What's hard is spotting the problem in the first place. Read what you write!

☞ **Overworking a vowel sound.**

> This conference offers an optimum opportunity to cost out promising software.

The proliferation of short *o* sounds is likely to take a reader's mind off the content of your sentence. Rewrite:

> You'll have an excellent chance to price attractive software at this conference.

☞ **Breaking into rhythm or rhyme.** As I mentioned, business writers shouldn't write poetry. You want to be known for your lean, terse prose. That means editing to control this sort of thing:

> We see all three in the '03 fee.

> Sell Morrell and O'Dell will rebel.

> Our income is well diversified, small banking business aside.

Let's see. How about

> All three of these changes are reflected in the fee schedule for 2003,

> If we put the Morrell division up for sale, we'll get resistance from O'Dell.

and

Apart from our small banking business, our income is well diversified.

As always, the problem is easy to see and hear in someone else's work, hard to recognize in your own. Keep reminding yourself as you revise, and *listen* to what you've written.

—— THE BOTTOM LINE ——

- **Avoid beginning several words in a sentence with the same letter.**

- **Rewrite to edit out an oversupply of one vowel sound.**

- **Guard against creating accidental rhythms or rhymes.**

CHAPTER 11

HAVE I VENERATED THE SACRED COWS OF WRITING?

G.K. Chesterton said, "There are three rules of good writing, and nobody knows what they are." There are, however, a few rules that everybody seems to know. Interestingly enough, historically these rules haven't always been observed, nor is there general agreement that they are justified. In some cases, there's not even a legitimate grammatical or logical reason for them. Nevertheless, if enough people are convinced of something, for all practical purposes it becomes a rule.

Because I believe in writing defensively and not stirring anybody up if I don't have to, I try to observe these rules—as long as it doesn't cause me pain or do violence to my sentence structure. I strongly suggest you do the same in the following areas. Why lay yourself open to criticism, justified or not? The cows follow.

☞ **Don't split infinitives.** The infinitive form of a verb is *to* and whatever: to wait, to invite, to promote. Since in Latin this form is expressed in one word, some 19th century grammarians decided that these two parts of English verbs should not be split by an adverb, such as *really*: to *really* know. Since English is not Latin, nor even a Romance language, I don't think that's much of a justification for the rule. It does, however, make sense in certain cases where the two verb halves are widely split and a misreading is possible. For example:

> She has agreed *to* with much enthusiasm in the future *search* for a new account manager.

You can see that *to search* gets lost as a verb because the split is so wide, and it's possible to read *future search* incorrectly as a noun. An infinitive split such as *to quickly move*, or *to simply ask*, on the other hand, seems relatively harmless.

Authors of style manuals unanimously agree there are many things worse than a split infinitive, including stilted and obvious efforts to avoid one, but for some reason people remember the no-splitting rule from grade school. I knew a CEO who got a sharply critical letter from the same customer every time his huge retail organization split an infinitive in promotional copy—ads, direct mail, etc.—as if the CEO were personally responsible for each of the splits. Since he happened to know a lot about language and writing, but couldn't keep an eye on all company copywriters, this infuriated him. Clearly, people not only remember the rule, they *like* remembering it and enjoy criticizing people who fail to observe it. Since I can't afford to have people criticizing my grammar, I always rephrase to avoid a split. Since you can't afford it either, go ahead and rewrite to reconnect or eliminate a split infinitive. It's almost always easy.

I'd like you *to generally brief* the consultant on our progress to date.

Here you can probably omit the splitter, *generally*, which adds little substance anyhow.

Was it wise *to conveniently "forget"* his prison record?

A more interesting problem. *Conveniently* fits naturally where it is, not very comfortably elsewhere: I'm sure that's where one would place it in a conversation. Yet to avoid the appearance of incorrect writing, I'd rewrite. There are plenty of ways to do this:

I question the wisdom of conveniently "forgetting" his prison record.

Was it wise to "forget" his prison record so conveniently?

You've conveniently "forgotten" his prison record. Is that wise?

☞ **Never end a sentence with a preposition.** This means concluding with one of those little words, often words of location: *over, under, around, in.* "Preposition overhang" slides by easily in conversation, and it feels natural: "This company has nothing to be ashamed of"; "I've forgotten what I came for." When you write, you may have a problem, because your boss, or your reader, may perceive it as incorrect. Here are two more examples of preposition overhang:

I can't decide which slide to end *with*.

The senior account executive justifiably resents having been lied *to*.

Historical precedents abound for ending sentences with prepositions. Shakespeare did it in Hamlet's soliloquy, citing "The heartache and the thousand natural shocks/That flesh is heir to…" Our forefathers did it. Here's Benjamin Franklin: "Do not squander time, for that's the stuff life is made of." Churchill is said to have famously growled that the supposed rule was "the sort of English up with which I will not put," illustrating the potentially stilted results of observing it. As for current examples, that pundit of the proper, former *National Review* editor William J. Buckley, says in his book, *The Right Word*, "It is not a sign of arrogance for the king to rule. That is what he is there for." And English playwright Alan Bennett writes in *Writing Home*, "One of the exercises in rehearsal required each member of the cast to…shout out at the top of his voice the worst thing he could think of."

To this distinguished crowd, ending with a preposition is clearly no sin at all. In the 1700s, however, John Dryden, "probably on the basis of a specious analogy to Latin," notes the *American Heritage Dictionary* (those Romans again), invented the rule against

ending with a preposition. Heady times for sure, when the poet lau-
reate gets to go around making up grammar rules: I missed my
century. I will concede that you can get some unlovely sentences
ending in prepositions, which is probably why Dryden thought up
his rule. Here's another famous, probably fictional, example. The
young child says to the parent:

> What did you bring that book I didn't want to be
> read *to out of up for*?

Five prepositions in a row, and the effect is predictably nasty.
But more to the point, plenty of people learned that ending with
a preposition is not just awkward, it's *wrong*. So, if you can comfortably rewrite so as to avoid flouting this rule, even though it's
based on a "specious premise," why not?

> I can't decide which slide to use in conclusion.

> The senior account executive justifiably resents the
> lies she was told.

Use your ingenuity to block potential criticism of preposition overhang.

☞ **Don't begin a sentence with a conjunction, such as
and or *but*.** Again, it's the amorphous "they" who say you
mustn't do it. We can only speculate about where this one got

going. The authors of the Bible, the framers of the Constitution and the Bill of Rights, and Abraham Lincoln were all apparently unaware of this injunction and began sentences with *and, or, so, for*, etc., with impunity. And if they weren't divinely inspired, who is?

> And God said, Let there be light: and there was light.
>
> —Genesis 1:1

> But in a larger sense, we cannot consecrate, we cannot hallow…
>
> —Abraham Lincoln, the Gettysburg Address

Most reputable grammarians call the rule nonsense, and I have trouble with it, too: it seems particularly capricious and ill-founded. In fact, you can find sentences beginning with *and, or*, and *but* throughout this book: but that's primarily because I knew I'd have a chance to explain on this page. I'd advise you, particularly if you're trying hard to please, to edit out starting conjunctions—unless you're quite confident your reader (or your boss) is not a grammar freak, or you're writing very informally. Starting with conjunctions flies well, for example, in ad copy:

> We'll give you the first six issues free! *But* that's not all! You won't be charged an annual fee. *And* your finance charge will be just 1.1 percent, so you'll save even more.

☞ **Avoid beginning a sentence with however.** Who thought up this loser? "They" again. But since a number of people are convinced it's correct, get along by going along. It's perfectly simple to move the word from the head of the sentence to some more innocuous place:

> *However*, I feel that the technical superiority of the product more than offsets the higher cost.
>
> I feel, *however*, that the...

Obviously, where all these sacred cows are concerned, I belong to the Neville Chamberlain school of grammar: peace at any price.

—— THE BOTTOM LINE ——

- **Why risk offending picky readers? Embrace your inner appeaser and write out**

    - **split infinitives**

    - **sentences that end with for, of, or some other preposition**

    - **sentences that start with and, but, or some other conjunction**

    - **sentences that start with however**

CHAPTER 12

HAVE I DEALT CAREFULLY WITH PRONOUNS?

Pronoun problems are a grammar issue, which means there are clear rules about right and wrong, and pronouns can be tricky. They are virtually all we have left of English as the inflected language it once was: English word endings used to change, like those of Latin, depending on how the word was used in a sentence. Today's English mercifully doesn't do that, except for these small, important words. That's why we have three forms for most pronouns: *he* for the subject, or doer of the action, *him* for the object, the receiver of the action (including objects of prepositions), and *his* for the possessive, the owner of whatever. Here they are, for the record:

	SUBJECT	OBJECT	POSSESSIVE
Singular	I	me	mine
	you	you	yours
	he, she, it	him, her, it	his, hers, its
	who	whom	whose
Plural	we	us	ours
	you	you	yours
	they	them	theirs
	who	whom	whose

The words in the left-hand column substitute for the initiator of action: John/*He* hit the wall. Those in column 2 are for the receiver of action: The nature of the error hit Sarah/*her*. Those in the third express possession; they take the place of belonging to a person or persons, etc.: The book is John and Sarah's/The book is *theirs*.

In a conversation, you can usually get away with making pronoun errors—unless, of course, you are speaking with a fastidious person who hates "Between you and I." If you are writing, however, you document an error clearly and more or less permanently.

To escape this fate, here are my suggestions for cleansing your work of the most jarring and incorrect pronoun mistakes.

☞ **Note that the possessive pronouns take NO apostrophes.** We normally make possessive forms by adding an apostrophe or an apostrophe and *s*. Not to pronouns. Never, never. As I mentioned, they're old forms, and they're irregular. You will never be called upon to write *your's*, *her's*, *it's* (in the sense of *belonging to it*), or *their's*. You can comfortably assume that for all practical purposes these words simply *don't exist* (in

certain cases, a linguist might need them, but I can't conceive of needing them in business writing).

☞ **Scrutinize pronoun pairs for case agreement.** How often have you heard, from the mouths of babes, as it were, "Her and me want to go to the mall"? I hope not very. Interestingly, surely not even the worst offenders would say, "*Her* wants to go" or "*Me* want to go." The trouble occurs when a pronoun is *paired* with another pronoun, or a noun, as in "*Janet and me* want to go." So the fix is easy: simply make sure each pronoun is correct alone. If you have written

> The lawyer requested postponement of the court date for *John and I*,

separate *I* from *John*. Now try reading the sentence:

> ...postponement of the court date for *I*.

Oops. If it doesn't work without *John*, it's incorrect with him. "John and *me*" is correct. Here's another:

> *He and she* started work in this office in September 2005.

Divide and conquer: "*He* started," "*She* started." That sentence is fine as written.

It's the same for such constructions as "*Us Tareyton smokers* would rather fight than switch," a cigarette ad that upset a few grammarians, amateur and professional, back in the day. Again, just separate the two elements, *Us* and *Tareyton smokers*. "*Us* would rather fight"? Me don't think so. "*We* Tareyton smokers." Here's another example:

> The accountant asked *we consultants* about our expense reports.

Split 'em up: "The accountant asked *we*..." Not good. "*Us* consultants" is correct. With this exercise of unpairing, you can solve The Case of the Paired Pronouns, every time.

☞ **Make sure your pronouns agree in number with the subject they represent.** A pronoun is a stand-in for someone or something previously mentioned:

> *Julia* is a Chartered Financial Analyst. *She* got her degree at Brandeis.

Simply put, we don't say "Julia...he" or "Julia...they." Clear enough. Problems arise at least in part, I suspect, as a result of many women's refusal to accept the time-honored *he* as a generic reference to a person of unknown gender. This makes people want to say "When the new manager comes aboard, *they*," which may be politically correct but is grammatically unconscionable. See Chapter 15 for some easy and grammatical fixes that will pass the scrutiny of the PC police.

☞ **Department of Details. Watch out for three frequently misused pronouns:**

1. **myself**: Two good uses for this pronoun include emphasis:

   I *myself* was unable to make the trip, but our senior vice president went.

   and reflexivity, which means doing something to oneself:

   I asked *myself* why I had established *myself* in this backwater town.

   Bad uses include using *myself* as a substitute for *I* or *me*:

   Steve and *myself* will stop by your desk once you're settled.

She wanted Mike and *myself* to provide detail on the systems conversion.

Using *myself* in this way, as the *American Heritage Dictionary*'s Usage Panel comments, in one of its notes, "can indicate pomposity or a sense of importance." Do you want people to think you're that kind of person? Not I myself! (Besides, I admire the Usage Panel extravagantly—it includes William Safire, Anne Tyler, John Simon, Jeane Kirkpatrick, Arthur M. Schlesinger, Jr., William Zinsser, and nearly 200 other smart, literate people, so its collective opinion rates high with me.)

2. **who** and **whom**: Calvin Trillin says the word *whom* was invented to make everyone sound like a butler. In other words, snootier than thou. That's pretty cute, and I'll concede he has a point. But we still need *whom* as well as *who* in our writing. Our language is not so debased that we can't remember, at least in writing, to distinguish between the subject and the object pronoun. Write *who* if you'd write *she*. Write *whom* if you'd write *her*. It's simple enough, though you may have to do a little shuffling of word order, because the *who/whom*s often throw their part of a sentence into the order of a question, whether the sentence is an actual question or not. Let's try a couple of examples:

I interviewed the woman *who/m* you recommended.

Substitute *she* you recommended, then invert the order: you recommended *she*—uh oh. Clearly that's wrong. *Her* you recommended, you recommended *her*. Equally clearly, that's right. Therefore the word you should use is *whom.*

Try this one:

Who/m is the best technician on your team?

He is the best technician? Exactly. Use *who.*

An aside on the spoken word. Some people, apparently going Mr. Trillin one better, believe that *whom* has the upper-crust sound of an *English* butler and is therefore to be preferred on all occasions. (It's part of the American inferiority complex that makes us compulsively watch Masterpiece Theater and think anyone with an English accent sounds smart.) You will sound like a very ungrammatical butler if you go around asking on the telephone, "*Whom* shall I say is calling?" Substitute another pair of pronouns: *She* is calling or *her* is calling? It's *who.* Incidentally, "May I tell him who is calling?" avoids the problem. I don't even like to ask who's calling: my mother told me it's rude, but we're dealing with the business word, not the gentle South where she learned manners.

3. **who-** and **whomever**: If you want to use these words—and I'm not saying you must if you don't want to—you should know there's a trick involved, case-wise. (My friend Connie, who objects to *–wise*— see Chapter 6—is far from alone. Connie-wise, I'm behaving badly.) Their usage depends, once again, on whether the word is functioning as a subject or an object pronoun. The pronoun *whoever*, like *who*, stands for the subject, the initiator of the action, while *whomever* is, like *whom*, the object or recipient of action. Most of the time you can decide just as with *who* and *whom*, by substituting a more familiar pair of pronouns, such as *he* and *him*:

> *Whoever* wants it can have the Windsor account.

Because the type of pronoun that could substitute for who(m)ever is a subject pronoun—*he* wants, not *him* wants—the correct word is *whoever*.

> The children begged *whomever* they saw to take them swimming.

Substitute *he* or *him*: they saw *him*, therefore *whomever*.

But trouble comes with a sentence such as this:

Mrs. Tilledge shows *who(m)ever* visits the store her horrible-looking grandchildren's pictures.

Whoever is correct here, as it's the subject of the verb "visits," (*he* visits, *we* visit), but "shows *whoever*" rightly bothers people who are inclined to dwell on things. Shouldn't *whoever* be the *object* of the verb "shows"? In which case, wouldn't "shows *whomever*" be correct, just as you'd say "shows *me*" or "shows *him*"? An excellent question.

The key to this puzzle is that *whoever* is leading a bigamous double life. It is simultaneously both the object of what comes *before* it, Mrs. Tilledge's showing, and the subject of what comes *after*, the visiting. As some grammar books put it, the word "squints" in both directions. This can make it hard to determine at a glance whether you should use *whoever* or *whomever*.

Here is a simple way to get it right every time. Give yourself a "shadow" person to operate as the object of whatever may come before: say Harvey, Jimmy Stewart's imaginary rabbit. Or your sister, or The Artist Formerly Known as Prince. Who(m)ever. Then, when you're uncertain whether to use *whoever* or *whomever*, substitute "Harvey, *who*" or Harvey, *whom*." *Who*, remember, is the subject, the *I/he/they* pronoun case, *whom* the object, or *me/him/them* one.

You may not want to think too hard about this—just do it. It's 100 percent effective:

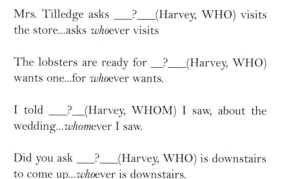

Mrs. Tilledge asks ___?___(Harvey, WHO) visits the store...asks *who*ever visits

The lobsters are ready for ___?___(Harvey, WHO) wants one...for *who*ever wants.

I told ___?___(Harvey, WHOM) I saw, about the wedding...*whom*ever I saw.

Did you ask ___?___(Harvey, WHO) is downstairs to come up...*who*ever is downstairs.

Having gone on at some length about this issue, I tardily recollect that I told you you never, ever have to use *who(m)ever* if it makes you unhappy. Mrs. Tilledge could just as easily show "everybody who visits," lobsters are ready "if you want one," "I told everyone I saw," and you can "ask the guests downstairs to come up." Edit the pesky pair out of your writing entirely, if you like. If you do use them, however, use them correctly.

Attention to these highlights in the secret life of pronouns should keep you more or less entirely out of trouble.

—— THE BOTTOM LINE ——

- Be aware that pronouns change form depending on their use in your sentence.

- Remember that possessive pronouns (*its, theirs,* etc.) take no apostrophes.

- Unpair nouns and pronouns to be sure your pronoun's in the right case.

- Make sure a pronoun agrees with its subject in number (not everybody…they).

- If you use them, pay special attention to *myself, who(m),* and *who(m)ever.*

CHAPTER 13

AM I MAKING BAD OR GOOD USE OF REPETITION?

When there's a reason for it, repetition can be an effective aid to communication.

☞ **Use repetition to reinforce a message.** As a rhetorical device, repetition can help make a message powerful and memorable. It's a time-honored tradition that dates from the Bible and the classics:

> Blessed are the poor in spirit, for theirs is the kingdom of heaven.
>
> Blessed are they that mourn, for they shall be comforted.
>
> Blessed are the meek, for they shall inherit the earth.
> —Matthew 5: 1–3

> A horse, a horse! my kingdom for a horse!
> —*Richard III*, iv, 7

Repetition can reinforce a message with considerable strength. During the Battle of Britain in World War II, Winston Churchill made use of it in speeches that inspired and encouraged his countrymen in England's "darkest hour":

> We shall fight them on the beaches; we shall fight on the landing grounds, we shall fight in the fields and in the streets, we shall fight in the hills; we shall never surrender.

You can make repetition work for you in business writing also, if less dramatically:

> We can improve our visibility by targeting proper market segments. We can improve our sales volume by increased efforts among Fortune 1000 companies. And we can improve delivery by making the best use of our distribution channels.

☞ **Use repetition to contribute to clarity.** It makes a certain amount of sense to identify things—be they systems, new projects, products, whatever—using the same word, to assure that readers understand you. It's definitely better than selecting a synonym no one understands. I read some direct mail copy from a bank that referred to checks, then to "demand deposit forms." I had no idea you could call a check that, and neither do most people. Your word of first choice may well be the best, anyway: there's a reason why you chose it first, after all. Especially if you're writing about something new or unfamiliar, using the same word to refer to it is a service to your readers.

> Remove the lock on the reverse side of the *keyboard.*
> Use the coiled cord to connect the *input device* to the
> 686SX terminal.

If I think about it, I can deduce that the input device must be the keyboard—but I don't want to *have* to think about it. I'd rather the instructions read *keyboard* in both places.

Do not under any circumstances be deceived into thinking you must come up with a new synonym each time for literary reasons. Students in what I call the Chronologically Challenged Tiny Person School of Writing will tie themselves in knots inventing one synonym after another, increasingly preposterous, for an ordinary word such as "baby." Come on. You are not Shakespeare, and you are not writing *King Lear.* You're a business writer conveying information. The contrived synonyms aren't really any more euphonious anyway, in most cases; in fact, they're usually so obvious as to be distracting. If it's a baby, keep calling it a baby. There's nothing inelegant or illiterate about that kind of repetition.

On the other hand, don't risk alienating your audience by *needlessly* repeating an idea or word. Redundancy is bad repetition because it's pointless and slipshod. Some oblivious writers raise redundancy to an art form. For example, "You're invited to repeat your presentation again" is apt only if the presentation has been made twice already. *Innovative new idea* means *new new idea.* And I have just about given up fighting the advertising folks who want to direct-mail *free gifts* to the public. If it isn't *free*, it isn't much of a gift. (Actually, given the kinds of Trojan horses most of these gifts turn out to be—a credit card free of annual fees[for now], a subscription with "no obligation," and so forth, all with unpleasant side effects—my point may be moot.) Here are some redundancies to avoid in your writing:

advance planning	join together
at this moment in time	must first be preceded
basically and funda- mentally	mutual cooperation
	other alternative
both…as well as	past history
consensus of opinion	repeat again
cooperate together	small in size
first and foremost	the reason why is because
free of charge	
future projections	two different kinds
general overview	usual custom
inadvertent error	X:00 a.m. in the morning
initially begin	
in X years from now	X:00 p.m. in the afternoon
innovative new	

Check carefully to be sure you've used repetition to reinforce and communicate, rather than simply to bloat your piece with unnecessary words.

—— THE BOTTOM LINE ——

- Use repetition as a rhetorical device to reinforce your message.

- For clarity, repeat your word of choice instead of contriving synonyms.

- Don't repeat pointlessly: avoid redundant words and phrases.

CHAPTER 14

HAVE I USED PARALLEL CONSTRUCTION FOR CORRECTNESS AND CHARM?

In Chapter 13 we discussed repetition of words or phrases as an aid to communicating your message. Repetition of *form*, or parallel construction, can help deliver a strong message as well. Parallelism is the doctrine that says if you're using words or phrases in a sentence in the same way, they should be equivalent in form for appeal and effect. In other words, it's better to write

> John is helpful, hardworking, and reputable.

than

> John is helpful, a man who works hard, and of good reputation.

The three adjectives in the first example are parallel in form.

In the second series, John *is* all three things. Yet because the first is an adjective, the second a noun form, and the third a prepositional phrase, the sentence, though grammatically correct, is awkward and lacking in style.

☞ **Parallel elements make your message strong and appealing.** Parallel construction is a device used by speechmakers, often combined with apt word repetition, to deliver points with eloquence and style. Abraham Lincoln used it to magnificent effect. The Gettysburg Address, depending on how you count, contains at least 17 examples of parallelism, of which the most famous is probably "government of the people, by the people, and for the people." What if Lincoln had said "populist government, people-driven, and for the people"? I'm guessing it wouldn't have made *Bartlett's Familiar Quotations.*

☞ **Nonparallel can mean ungrammatical.** In some cases, the lack of parallel form results in ungrammatical or illogical combinations. This error, sometimes called a *false series*, is often the result of haste or halfway editing. Such bad stuff as the following can result:

> The company has installed a new cafeteria, a fitness center, and a modular conference center is being planned.

The writer apparently plans to list several new areas *the company has installed*, begins in style by listing two, then wanders off into a whole new clause. As a result, the sentence isn't really coherent. You can't *install a new modular conference center is being planned*, yet that's the third "item" listed.

The bad apple in the bunch isn't always the last in a series:

> You can use the automated teller machine (ATM) to get cash, deposits, and transfer funds.

Here the culprit is *deposits*. *Get cash* and *transfer funds* are matching items, verb forms following *to*. Alas, you can't *to deposits*.

Faulty parallels are often found in vertical listings:

> This afternoon's meeting agenda includes
> * reading the minutes of the last meeting
> * begin budget allocation
> * business plan for fiscal year '07-'08
> * we'll discuss vacation schedules

Only the first of the agenda items can actually be read with the sentence heading. That's careless, unattractive, and incorrect. We already know what your boss would have to say about this one.

☞ **"Go vertical" to identify nonparallel sentence elements.** How can you identify faulty parallels in your own writing? It's easy to spot and fix the problem in a vertical list, so let's start with one of those. Here's an agenda from the general manager's office:

Monday's meeting will feature
- a report by the Buildings and Grounds Committee
- a showing of our new recruitment video
- three short presentations on new markets
- Treasurer Freddie Folsom will provide a financial update

Our manager's assistant, who drafted this agenda, almost made it through Monday's agenda in style, but Freddie Folsom was his downfall. Look at the heading, *Monday's meeting will feature.* Everything that follows that heading must complement it, or join logically with it. In other words, you must be able to read the header aloud coherently with *every single part* of the list that follows.

The first three work fine: *Monday's meeting will feature a report by the Buildings and Grounds Committee* and so on. *Monday's meeting will feature Treasurer Freddie Folsom will provide a financial update,* however, is gibberish in my book and yours, too, if you're well rested and not too hassled. (That's important, as hasty writing is often at the root of faulty parallel structure.)

Let's move from a vertical list to a series. Editing out faulty parallels in a series isn't really difficult either: a similar principle applies. Take the sentence

The new LAN administrator is efficient, experienced, and does her job well.

Sentences that contain a series of whatever are actually lists in horizontal form. The heading of the sentence above, "The new LAN administrator is," introduces a series of three items describing the new employee. According to the doctrine of parallelism, these three should be expressed in the same form. To make the scheme perfectly clear, a good stratagem is actually to write the sentence in vertical list form. So let's "go vertical" with the sentence:

> The new LAN administrator is
> * efficient,
> * experienced, [and]
> * does her job well

The introductory phrase *The new LAN administrator is* obviously works with *efficient;* it works with *experienced;* but "The new LAN administrator *is does her job well* doesn't make sense. On the other hand, you can change that third phrase and say, *"is efficient, experienced, and good at her job."* Now the introductory phrase makes sense with all three items.

Another way to fix faulty parallelism is to change the introductory phrase itself. Suppose we change the phrase in this case to read, *The new LAN administrator…* Change the second of the three parallel items so they read

> is efficient
> has experience [and]
> does her job well

To make sure we've got this issue pinned to the mat, let's try putting another of the sentences criticized above into vertical list form:

You can use the automated teller machine (ATM) to
get cash, deposits, and transfer your funds.

We take it vertical to give ourselves the best visibility on the
items involved:

You can use the automated teller machine (ATM) to get
- cash
- deposits
- transfer your funds

Sorry, but you can't say that. You don't *to get deposits* or *to get
transfer your funds.*
Try another introduction:

You can use the automated teller machine to
- get cash
- deposits
- transfer your funds

Now we have only item that doesn't work: *deposits.* If we
alter that to read *make deposits,* we have a hit on our hands:

You can use the automated teller machine (ATM) to
- get cash
- make deposits
- transfer your funds

You can also change the introductory line and the last item so the sentence reads

> You can use the automated teller machine (ATM) for
> * cash withdrawals
> * deposits
> * fund transfers

Now all you have to do is write out in horizontal form any of the lists that read correctly, choosing whichever you like best. You may not need to put your sentence into a vertical list form each time you're uncertain. But it is a handy way to see, very clearly, what goes wrong in a nonparallel series. In any case, that's how it works.

Keep an eye on items of two, three, or more in your writing and raise your consciousness so you're able to recognize nonparallel structures when they pop up. Often this happens as the result of adding yet another piece of information to what's already written. When it does, your communication may suffer. If you find nonparallel constructions in your work, use this mental geometry to straighten them out.

—— THE BOTTOM LINE ——

* **Use parallel structure to give strength and appeal to your writing.**

* **Avoid the ungrammatical and/or illogical false series.**

* **Try listing items in a series vertically if you're not sure they're parallel.**

CHAPTER 15

WHAT'S MY OQ (OFFENSE QUOTIENT)?

Read this section carefully to avoid embarrassing your organization, your boss, and yourself. Read it also to avoid hurting other people's feelings.

I've touched elsewhere on the subject of not upsetting people, and I hope I've convinced you it's a good idea. In America today, unfortunately, not upsetting people is not easy. Lashed on by the proponents of political correctness, we've hit such a pitch of sensitivity that half our citizens are poised to be hurt and the other half are terrified of hurting them. It's so easy to offend someone along racial, ethnic, residential, gender, health, and sexual preference lines that it's a wonder anyone stumbles through a page of work clean. Press on regardless. But as you go, try not to make an issue of things one way or another: be politically correct, in other words, but not so noticeably that you appear strident or in-your-face to those who are tired of politically correct. Take as your mantra the aspiration of Ezra Tull in Anne Tyler's *Dinner at the Homesick Restaurant*: "I'm trying to get through life as a liquid," and slip on through as innocuously as you can.

I'll highlight a few spots where trouble can erupt and make some suggestions for slipping through. Let's begin with the issue of gender, since everybody has one and most people accordingly feel they have the right to an opinion.

☞ **Gender: titles and pronouns.** It makes practical sense to be gender tender. I think the issue is less of a hot button than it has been, and a lot of people as old as I am didn't really care in the first place. But you never know. So especially if you're writing to an unknown person or audience, it pays to try not to annoy in either direction. You don't know whether you've got a diehard feminist on your hands or a Marabel Morgan (the woman who wrote about putting on babydoll pajamas and greeting her hubby at the door with a martini).

Take social titles: specifically, the Ms./Mrs./Miss by which you address female persons. Women sometimes call me in a snit— in snits, I suppose—because I've referred to them in an in-house newsletter I write for as *Ms.* They are *Mrs.* Smith, they want me to know, and they hope I will be able to remember that henceforth, and so on in the same vein. Others call in snits, as you can probably guess, because I called them *Miss.* Don't I realize that this outmoded label is offensive in the workplace? What business is anyone's marital status to anyone else? Do men have a title that shows whether *they* are married? And so on. As I said, you never know.

By all means avoid using the pronouns *he*, *his*, and *him* when referring to an unspecified person or a category: "The customer service rep asks *his* callers…" But you can err on the other side of this conundrum as well. The *Mrs.* Smith crowd, as you might expect, tend to view *him or her* with a jaundiced eye, as a kowtow to the angry Mses. Even those who don't much care find it bulky and distracting, especially if it's repeated. I won't take sides on the issue, but such awkward and obvious constructions as *he/she*, *s/he*, or *he and she*, especially when used repeatedly, are really distracting. The alternative, too often, is a default to the plural, generic *they/them/their*, yielding such incorrect and unlovely stuff as

> When *a student* turns 19, *they* are no longer eligible for a free checking account.

> A new *staff member* often asks if *they* may be included in peer support training.

I appreciate the wish to be gender-sensitive that prompts these errors, but that doesn't make them any less wrong. The solution is to run around the issue using several helpful tricks. Try instead:

> **Plural:** When students turn 19, they are no longer...

> **Second person:** When you turn 19, you are no longer...

> **Rewrite:** A student who turns 19 is no longer...

☞ **Gender: occupations and positions.** Again, watch out for assumptions. Don't write as if you're surprised by *any*one's job: *woman doctor, woman lawyer* imply—a pretty outdated implication, by the way—that these professions are unusual for a woman. By the same token, *male nurse* and *male exotic dancer* imply these are the sole province of females. One lawyer tells an endearing story that shows just how far this country has come. Her kindergartner came home one day beaming. "Good news, Mom!" he said. "I found out today guys can be lawyers!"

So remember that he may be a day care provider, she a heliarc welder. She may be the boss; he may be the secretary. (And nobody sends *anybody* for coffee: it's just too risky.) Here's some suggested language for writing inoffensively about jobs:

NO	**YES**
chairman	chair, chairperson
Men Working	Work in Progress
repairman	service representative, technician
salesman	salesperson
spokesman	spokesperson

Speaking of jobs, be aware that the word *employee* has come under fire from the thought police recently. They think it has a demeaning sound and prefer more euphemistic terms, such as *staff, staff member, workers,* or *people.* Ironically, the word *employee* itself was originally a euphemism for the word *servant.* And so we move onward, though the direction of our progress may be in doubt.

☞ **Gender: vocabulary.** Some feminists dislike words that reflect, or appear to reflect, historical masculine dominance. If you can do so without it being so obvious as to offend *non*feminists, substitute

workhours	for	man-hours
courageously	for	manfully
face to face	for	man to man
resources	for	manpower
synthetic	for	manmade
the human race	for	mankind
operating	for	manning

I have a little trouble with this category, and so do some other readers. It seems so—well, small. And being told a word is off limits smacks of censorship. So again, try to make your substitutions unobtrusive. Above all, don't go radical and start writing about *herstory, womanual,* and *perone* (*per* + *one*: not *son*—guess why). That's nonsense that doesn't advance anybody's interests. Besides, these words are derivatively unsound.

☞ **Gender: names.** Many names can belong to a person of either sex. For some reason, their owners feel you should know their gender intuitively, and they tend to be humorless and unhelpful about the issue. So, to avoid offending when you must write "Dear Mr." or "Dear Ms." to Lee, Campbell, Cameron, or J. B., hustle around and find out whether it's a boy or a girl. I sometimes call up on some pretext or other: whoever answers the phone usually gives it away without being asked.

Of course, if you have a mailing list of 1,000 customers, this doesn't work. In such cases, you're better off with "Dear Lee Rogers" or "Dear M. S. Jones." "Dear Sir or Madam" works under some circumstances, but it has a legalistic flavor that may not suit your text.

While I'm at it, don't be too quick to get on a first-name basis.

Older people, especially, may view this as just plain rude. Know what? As I hurtle toward old-personhood, I'm starting to agree.

☞ **Racial or ethnic group.** I try to avoid labeling, in honor of the fact that we are all primarily people, and also because labels change so fast. For the record, here's what's considered inoffensive in America today; don't hold me to it tomorrow:

People of Spanish/American descent	Hispanic
People of Latin-American descent	Latino
People of African descent	African American
People of Asian descent	Asian American
North American indigenous population	Native American or Native American Indian

Watch out for racial or ethnic expressions that may wound or insult. In conversation you may not realize a mistake until it's too late, and people tend to make allowances and accept a sincere apology. But in writing there are few excuses. And there is no excuse at all for the woman in whose prepared speech as part of a school building dedication I heard, with disbelief, "I didn't think we had a Chinaman's chance in hell of getting the building finished by May." Say—shouldn't that be "Chinaperson's"? Whatever, her largely Asian and Asian American student audience collectively gave, to put it mildly, a sharp intake of breath. On their behalf, so did the rest of us.

Guard against making assumptions in your writing that exclude or simply don't apply to certain groups. The *Boston Globe*'s use of the expression "bled white by war," for example, was criticized in a letter to the editor, because many Americans don't get white when they bleed. I've heard "tickled pink" faulted for the same reason: not everyone's pink, tickled or not. Supersensitive? You bet. Worth honoring? You bet your life.

☞ **Designations that highlight age.** *Kids*, *teens*, *elders*, and *seniors* are labels that can offend members of those groups also. Not to mention mislabeled nonmembers: it can be dangerous to make assumptions in this context. A friend who markets a highly competitive sports software product was wining and dining four industry principals, men in their early 30s. She's 62, but hardly looks it; she's vivacious and enormously attractive for any age. Cocktails and witty conversation flowed, she was persuasive and charming, the young men responded, and she was expecting to close the deal by dessert, when the waitress asked her, "Would you like to see the senior citizens' menu?" My friend didn't lose the business as a result, but she did lose face, and the waitress lost a tip. Don't make such a howler in writing. Think twice, print once.

☞ **Terms that pertain to physical impairment.** My recommendation is to check with the person or group in question. Most are very specific about what they wish to be called. People who have hearing problems, for example, prefer to be known as "hearing impaired people and the deaf," referring, respectively, to those with a lesser or more profound hearing loss. Descriptive terms for many conditions have given way to scientific or medical terms: a person who was called Mongoloid a generation ago is more aptly referred to today as a person with Down or Down's Syndrome. Note also a tendency to label a disease, condition, or injury, rather than a person: hence, "He has mental retardation" rather than "He is retarded."

If you didn't know all this before, you're probably trembling. Join the club (open to everyone). Yes, it's a minefield out there, and we must tread carefully. Don't tell anyone, but occasionally I wish I'd lived in the Bad Old Days, when you automatically called someone with a glass eye Squinty. Sort of clears the air. My father knew a man everybody called Charley Go Hump because he ended each sentence with "hump." Definitely not a politically correct name, but Dad said Charley didn't seem to mind: he realized the intent was humorous and affectionate. That's probably the heart of the issue—you need to be sure you'll come across as you intend. Maybe we don't know each other well enough nowadays to risk it—well, not in writing, anyway.

—— THE BOTTOM LINE ——

- **Write sensitively to avoid offending around gender issues**
    - **titles and pronouns**
    - **occupations and positions**
    - **vocabulary choices**
    - **names**

- **Avoid discriminating by racial or ethnic group.**

- **Avoid labels that highlight age.**

- **Use appropriate language for physical impairments.**

CHAPTER 16

HAVE I MAINTAINED THE SUBJECT-VERB CONNECTION?

Here's an incredibly easy way to help ensure that your prose communicates. Be certain your subjects stay as close to their verbs as possible without making your sentences sound weird or stilted. Thus *office equipment remains, John was sent, vacations are, the vice president announced*, etc. Not *the vice president, perhaps unduly influenced by his assistant, with whom he was having an extraoffice romance, announced....*You'll lose your readers as you saunter toward the action, your verb. They may never find out *what* the vice president did, other than canoodle with a coworker, and they may not care. That's a chance you cannot afford to take. Don't separate subjects and verbs unless you have to, and if you have to, make the split as small as possible.

One way to remember to practice this rule is to think of the two parts of speech as the two halves of a seat belt: buckle up for safety. As you write and when you edit, watch for these pairs and try not to separate them any more than you must:

The new *programmer seems* both pleasant and competent.

When the meeting ended at noon, *everyone felt* encouraged by the progress we'd made.

Especially in the kind of information-rich writing you do, it's tempting to insert another fact, add another descriptive phrase, include modifiers in the name of litigation. Tempting, and awfully easy, too, thanks to Word and its colleagues. But overenthusiastically practicing this technique tends to clog up the works. When you separate the subject, the initiator in your sentence, from its action, the verb, a sentence emerges that's likely to be confusing, sometimes even ungrammatical. For example:

The new regulation replacing the older ones referring to formica counters the principles of free enterprise.

Anyone besides me misread the sentence, if only briefly, as discussing formica counters? As I've said before, it isn't nice to mislead your reader. Here's another:

Our *president*, with his three vice presidents, and thanks to his able board of directors, *are prepared* to carry this merger forward.

Doubtless the writer would never have said in cold blood, "Our president are. . ." But as he or she added bits of information, the subject became separated from its verb so widely, and so many bodies got into the act, that it was easy to misconstrue the subject as plural. As a result, our writer wound up not only creating a sprawling, unclear sentence but committing a grammatical error (see Chapter 17 on agreement—*with* doesn't create a plural). All that information can certainly be included if it's important—but it needs to be repackaged:

> Thanks to encouragement from the board of directors and his three vice presidents, the *president is prepared* to carry this merger forward.

or perhaps

> Thanks to encouragement from the board of directors, *the president and his three vice presidents are prepared* to carry this merger forward.

The moral is simple. The more material you compress into the subject-verb cranny, the more likely you are to forget just what your subject *is*. Keep the cranny narrow, the way crannies are supposed to be.

I'm not saying you should never put a modifying clause between your subject and verb. Variety demands it, as does the need to get a lot of information across efficiently. For instance:

The *manager* who asked for time off *has been fired.*

Beth Piper, taking the annual income projections in turn, *explained* how they had been developed.

No confusion is likely. Nor am I talking about inserting an adverb where it falls naturally:

Brian simply *forgot* that the meeting had been rescheduled.

Trying to put *simply* somewhere else (Brian forgot *simply?* *Simply* Brian forgot? Brian is simple?) to satisfy the rule spoils the sentence while it clouds meaning. That's the worst of both worlds. No, I'm talking big, ugly splits. To the extent you're dealing with complex material, and if you've inserted more than one modifier between subject and verb, you should consider revising: you may be headed for trouble. Here's another example:

The Bostech *customer service rep*, whether through slow call answering, poor listening skills, or inattention to detail, sometimes *annoy* customers.

In this case, *customer service rep* refers to Bostech reps as a whole or group; with that mindset, and given the wide split before the verb, the writer understandably forgot having written *rep*, not *reps*.

Understandably, but not excusably. You're responsible for your work. That means rereading, and possibly rewriting, to maintain the connection between the actor and the action. I check my copy, especially if my subject is complex or I sense that the writing lacks clarity or grace, to see whether sentence subjects and verbs are sticking together. The more subject-verb pairs I can identify, the more I admire myself. For example, this chapter has sent my self-esteem sky high. Although I admit to editing and a certain degree of low cunning, you're reading a paragraph that contains six pairs of subjects and verbs in the main part of each sentence—*you're responsible, that means, I check, I admire, chapter has sent,* and *you're reading*—and seven more in clauses: *maintain the connection, subject is, I sense, writing lacks, subjects and verbs are, I can identify,* and *I admit.*

You can see for yourself that I've done the same thing pretty consistently throughout the chapter and in fact throughout the book. Like Brooke Shields and her Calvin Kleins, I try to let nothing, absolutely nothing, come between my subjects and my verbs. See that you do the same.

—— THE BOTTOM LINE ——

- **Keep your subject and verb connected closely if you can**

    - **to maximize clarity**

    - **to minimize mistakes**

CHAPTER 17

HAVE I ADDRESSED ISSUES OF AGREEMENT?

We've already talked about being sure pronouns agree with their subjects (Chapter 12). But other facets of agreement exist. The principle of agreement also requires that subjects and verbs agree in number: singular noun, singular verb. We say James *was*, James and Theo *were*. We say *he is*, *I was*. These forms are usually correct, but not always. In fact, the whole area is not always that easy to navigate. You can't always tell whether your subject is really a singular or a plural, and even if it's singular, certain verbs may require a change. Remember, discriminating people may be watching you. (It's my *job* to make you paranoid. Paranoid is just another word for highly aware.) High spots follow where you can pick up a friend or an enemy, depending on whether you're doing things right or wrong. Here are some handy rules to help you with the hard spots:

☞ **As well as, in addition to, and with.** These words don't create plural subjects, so the verb stays singular:

> *Mark*, as well as Susan, *is attending* the conference in Dallas.
>
> *Estelle*, with her four clients, has reserved the board room until 6:00 p.m.

In fact, if you bracket part of a group in commas, even with *and*, you've lost them as part of your subject. By using those commas, you identify them as incidental (see use of the comma in Chapter 18):

> *Jim*, and the rest of the board as well, *is* staying at the Ramada Inn.
>
> *Tanya*, not to mention her three clients, *is* furious at being kept waiting.

If the "extras" in commas are important enough to be part of the subject, then rewrite the sentence to include them: Jim and the rest of the board are staying, Sarah and her three clients are furious.

☞ **Rule with or and nor.** If the parts of a compound subject are joined by *or* or *nor*, the verb agrees with the subject closest to it:

> Neither Reed nor his partners *understand* the technology they purchased.

> The attorneys or the boss himself *plans* to view the signing.

☞ **Group or collective nouns.** Problems arise with "group" or collective nouns: Do we say "The staff *is*" or "the staff *are*"? "Management *is*" or "management *are*"? Surprisingly, the answer is yes. The rule is that when the word in question is being considered as a whole, we use a singular verb; when the word identifies things or people considered severally or as individuals, we use a plural one. In the following example, the staff operates as a unified group:

> The staff *is* opposed to a four-day, ten-hour work week.

In the example below, on the other hand, they are operating individually:

> The staff *are* bringing their daughters to work.

Note that you cannot recast *staff* in the singular in that sentence even if you want to without running into a significant problem. The staff is bringing its daughter?

> Management has *offered* a generous severance package.

Management *have revealed* hidden abilities in the talent show auditions.

Again, in most cases, if you're uncomfortable with the verb, you can easily rewrite:

The group *has/have* revealed *its/their* compassionate side in the recent dispute.

The group revealed a compassionate side in the recent dispute.

Among collective nouns, a few special cases exist that are worth mentioning:

-**Majority** and **percentage** are singular or plural depending on whether the collection is singular or plural:

A majority of *us are* voting against going public.

A large percentage of the town's *population is* Republican.

-*A* **number** of industrialists *are*, but ***the*** **number** of industrialists *is*.

English sure is fun! A grammar handbook or general style manual will help with a lot of these: *Words into Type* is particularly good.

☞ **Plural subjects treated as single nouns.** I suspect you know this convention and follow it automatically. When you are characterizing an amount of something, as distinguished from the several items involved—be it time, money, unit of measure, or people—you are correct in using a singular verb. The following sentences are therefore just right as they stand:

> *Five hours* without a break *seems* too long for any seminar.

> I asked for *ten customer service reps*, which *was* probably more than we needed.

> *Eighteen miles* is too far from Route 95 for a satellite office.

The recorded voice that tells me when I'm telephone banking that one hundred dollars have been transferred from my account to my son's account grates on me like screeching chalk: it's no use to scream into the phone, "Has been! has been!" She can't hear me. But it's a mistake, and other customers of my bank have mentioned it.

☞ **Words that trip some of the people some of the time.** Don't get stuck with an amateur writer label by getting any of these wrong. The following words always take singular verbs:

> **anybody, anyone** *is...*
> **each** (of us, of them) *shows...*
> **either, neither** (of the offices) *connects...*
> **every** (manager and staff member) *remembers...*
> **everybody, everyone** *asks...*
> **somebody, someone** *obliges...*
> **nobody, no one** *compares...*

None (of a group of countable persons or things) takes a singular verb if you mean *not one single one.* For example:

> We tested 19 applicants, but none *was* as skilled as Carolyn.

> I tried all the Xerox machines, but none *is* in working order.

And *none* is singular when it refers to a single, uncountable noun:

> None of the *software works* on this machine.

> None of the small business *market has* defected to our competition.

None is plural, however, when you mean not *any*:

> I've asked around, but none of our salespeople *are* going to Detroit.

> None of us *were* eager to hear about fourth-quarter earnings.

You may have heard a so-called rule that *none* is always a contraction of *no one* and must therefore always take a singular verb. This is one of those rules that come (not *comes:* see below) out of nowhere, like the suburban myth of the razor blade in the Halloween apple. No case of an apple with a razor blade in it has ever been documented, but the story spread like kudzu. Same with this none habit. All the authorities are with you on this one, so go ahead and fight back if your boss challenges you. Produce any reputable dictionary—an *American Heritage*, for example, or a *Merriam-Webster*—and you'll find the same call. Show the Big Burrito. Case closed.

☞ **Just one of those things.** The expression "one of those people who" or "one of those things that" is a useful phrase with a pleasantly conversational ring to it. Be sure, however, that you are not tricked into thinking the verb that follows should be singular, modifying *one*. It is plural, modifying the person or thing, like this:

Runner Alberto Salazar, on a Boston Marathon

defeat: "It's just one of those things that *happen.*"
The late Katherine Graham, former publisher of
the *Washington Post*, in her memoir: "Dad wrote
me…that he had had one of those lucky breaks that
sometimes *occur.*"

To see that the *that* clause in each case modifies the object of
the preposition *of* (*things* and *breaks*, in these examples), rather
than *one*, just invert the sentence order, which makes the logic
clear:

Of those *things that happen*, this is just one.

Of those *lucky breaks that sometimes occur*, he had had
one.

Yes, it's a small point. But the effect you create with your
writing is composed of a number of small points, any of which
could be the very thing that happens to bother your discriminating reader. Here are two more examples that demonstrate
why the plural is virtually always the correct choice after *one of*:

She is one of those people who really *enjoy* managing.

Of those people who really *enjoy* managing, she is one.

I am one of those investors who *are* comfortable
with moderate risk.

Of those investors who *are* comfortable…I am one.

If you're not convinced and still feel uneasy with the plural verb, or if someone to whom you report hassles you about it, remember that no one is making you use the construction. To slip through without offending, simply rewrite:

It's one of those things that can happen to anyone.

Dad had the kind of lucky break that sometimes occurs.

She is among those people who really enjoy managing.

As an investor I am comfortable with moderate risk.

☞ **Before you throw in the towel, consult your dictionary.**
A good dictionary can help you with issues of agreement, by designating a word as a collective noun that follows the rule for collective nouns given above, or by describing its idiosyncratic pattern. Dictionary examples are also helpful. Here's part of the definition of "politics" in my *American Heritage Dictionary:*

…*2. (used with a sing. or pl. verb. a.* The activities or affairs engaged in by a government, politician, or political party: *"All politics is local"* (Thomas P.

O'Neill, Jr.). *"Politics have appealed to me since I was
at Oxford because they are exciting morning, noon, and
night"* (Jeffrey Archer)....

The entry also includes a usage note that suggests ways to
determine whether politics should take a singular or plural
verb—in all, as thorough a treatment of the situation as you
could wish.

☞ **A word about the subjunctive mood.** *Judith be? I were?*
out of context, these sound like peculiarly virulent cases of subject-verb disagreement. Yet you've heard, read, and said them
before. These are examples of the subjunctive mood, which
causes verbs to behave differently from their usual selves.

In the 18th century, when Patrick Henry declaimed, "If *this
be* treason, make the most of it," the subjunctive mood was quite
common. We don't use it often today, but it has its moments.
You've been using it automatically since you were in grade
school, but it's useful to know the underlying rationale, should
you or a colleague experience a sudden desire to become one
with this funny tense. Two primary reasons exist today for
using the subjunctive:

1. Use the subjunctive mood with verbs of command-
   ing or requesting:

   Edward requested that *Judith and Ron be* ready to
   fly at a moment's notice.

I demand that *Jonathan return* every penny he stole.

I ask that *he remember* who gave him his start in this company.

2. Use the subjunctive to express a condition contrary to fact:

If *I were* sure he would retain all our staff, I'd gladly sell the shop. (But I'm not sure.)

If *she were* a kind person, I'd ask for help, but she's most unfeeling.

I'd help you if *it were* possible. (But it isn't.)

Do not, however, use the subjunctive for unknown outcomes or simple conditional sentences:

No: John asked if *I were* planning to join them.

Yes: John asked if *I was* going to join them.

No: Howard looked out to see if the *plane were* on the runway.

Yes: Howard looked out to see if the *plane was* on the runway.

If you abuse the subjunctive as in the examples above, to the well informed, you will sound incorrect; to the uninformed, like a smart aleck.

One final subjunctive-related issue. Subjunctive verbs describing a condition contrary to fact *in the past* look just like indicatives, our ordinary verbs, so we wouldn't need to discuss them at all except that for some reason people think the subjunctive is expressed *would have*:

> No: If he *would have told* me, I would have changed the prices immediately.

> Yes: If he *had told* me, I would have changed...

> No: If I *would have known* you were job-hunting, I would have promoted you immediately.

> Yes: If I had known you were job-hunting, I would have...

Maybe the *would have* in the second part of the sentence inspires some people to write *would have* in the first half: perhaps it's an effort to balance the two parts of the sentence and effect parallelism, but it's incorrect. You are *never* justified in writing c*ould have...would have*. Erase it from your mental hard disk in favor of the proper verb construction *had ...would have*.

That's about it, except for a few idiomatic phrases, such as "come what may" and "so be it." The subjunctive is increasingly rarely used today. But it's correct in these situations, and it lends a little elegance to your prose.

If you are unsure where the battle lines should be drawn on agreement, these rules should help you over the rough spots.

—— THE BOTTOM LINE ——

Avoid problems with agreement by following some important rules:

- *As well as, with,* **and** *in addition* **to don't create plural subjects.**

- **When** *or* **or** *nor* **links two or more subjects, the verb agrees with the subject closest to it.**

- **Miles, dollars, hours, etc., discussed as amounts take singular verbs.**

- **Watch for words that can trip you:** *each, everyone,* **etc. take singular verbs.**

- **It's "one of those people who** *are."*

- **Consult your dictionary.**

- **Use the subjunctive mood primarily in two situations.**

CHAPTER 18

HAVE I USED PUNCTUATION AS A GUIDE TO MEANING?

Here are the most important rules of punctuation as applied to business writing. If you follow them, you're unlikely to be misunderstood, and you won't vex people who like to see things done right. Like grammar rules, these are pretty inflexible. It's not a good idea to try to bend them: to make a convention effective and its meaning therefore unambiguous, everybody has to observe it.

I've listed the marks of which you should be most aware and the ways to use them—or not use them—so you'll be correct and clear. If you want more detail, see Kate Turabian's *Manual for Writers*, referenced in the back of this book.

☞ The comma (,)

The mark you'll need most frequently. Also the most frequently overused, to bad effect. The four major reasons for using the comma follow. There are others, certainly, but be attentive to these four and you'll strongly enhance your readability.

1. To distinguish items in a series of things or descriptive terms:

I met with Sam, Jane, and Thomas this morning.

She is smart, capable, and well informed.

If you learned in school that you may drop the final comma, start getting over it right now. This comma is the one that ensures you will not be misunderstood: it prevents misreading the last two items as a unit. Sometimes known as the serial comma, it's the choice of every good style manual going. Fidelity Vice Chairman Peter Lynch uses it, too. Here's a sentence from *Beating the Street*:

"In Sweden, it seemed that investors were underestimating the worth of Volvo, Skandia, and many other firms…"

I'll take his word for it about the stocks, but I know his punctuation is perfect.

Here's a line from an apocryphal will, drafted by a lawyer presumably since disbarred:
I hereby do give, bequeath, and devise my entire estate of $6,000,000 to be shared in equal amounts by my children Tom, Paul and Lily.

Most of us would assume that means $2 million per child. But because there is no comma between the names Paul and Lily, Tom argued—successfully, so says the story—that his father's intent was to leave half of the $6 million to him, and half to Paul and Lily, giving him $3 million and each of them a paltry $1.5 million. I think it's safe to say that Christmas was never the same for Tom and his siblings after that. Let's hope the extra million was worth it to him. Even if the story's not true, it's a great example of the power of punctuation and its capacity to render fine shades of meaning.

2. To set off an introductory clause of more than two or three words:

> To match our competitors' strength, we must market more aggressively.

> Watching our account executive's presentation, I was impressed by her knowledge.

You may omit the comma, though you don't have to, after a very short phrase:

> In 1990 (no comma) First United Bank called Porter-Acheson's commercial loans.

3. To separate independent clauses (same thing as two complete sentences, each with a subject and a verb) joined by *and*, *but*, *for*, *nor*, *so*, or *or*:

> I wish you could be with us, but I understand your reasons for refusing.

> We enjoyed visiting Parker Broadcasting, and we're impressed by your digitized telecasting capabilities.

Please remember that you can't leave out that *and* or other conjunction and simply connect with the comma. This is technically known as a run-on sentence or comma splice:

> No: Donna is invaluable, she helps with everything from bookkeeping to sorting coins.

Oh, sure, once in a while somebody gets away with it. Somebody like Julius Caesar, for instance, who, on his victory over the king of Pontus in 47 BC, connected three sentences with commas:

> Veni, vide, vici. (I came, I saw, I conquered.)

Note that Caesar was an emperor. Unless you are an actual emperor or have serious imperial aspirations, forget it.

Note also that you can*not* use a comma between two clauses complete with subject and verb and connected with *however, moreover, therefore, otherwise,* or *thus*: these are *not the same as and, but,* and the others above. They are adverbs, and they signal a sharp break that requires a semicolon:

    No: I wanted you to join us, however, I
        understand why you can't make it.

    Yes: I wanted you to join us; however, I
        understand…

4. To bracket certain "by the way" information (the sentence may need this information but can structurally stand without it):

    You were there, *in fact*, on the day we signed the contract with Wiggins.

    I asked you on Wednesday, *John*, to return the training video series.

    Thursday, *April 23, 1991*, was the date, *also*, of the TriCo, *Inc.*, annual meeting.

I supplied paper, pens, *etc.*, *i.e.*, all the materials needed for the class.

Note that such words and information, including *inc.*, the year, and all those little Latin abbreviations—i.e., e.g., etc.—are *bracketed at either end* by commas (unless they end a sentence and are followed by appropriate end punctuation). Don't stop with just one unless you're at the beginning or end of a sentence:

Yes: We were able, moreover, to capture market share in both quarters.

Yes: Moreover, we were able to capture market share in both quarters.

No: We were able, moreover to capture market share in both quarters.

No: We were able moreover, to capture market share in both quarters.

Remember that you are excerpting the "by the way" word or additional information: you demonstrate that by hooking the pair of commas around it.

Occasionally (don't take this as a license to start dropping commas everywhere) you may need to insert a comma to prevent a misreading. The follow-

ing sentence from a recent newspaper editorial
should have had one:

> The president is more confident about the
> regulatory uses of government, having proposed a
> consumers' bill of rights on managed care and
> flirting with a minimum wage hike.

A comma after "care" would have prevented my first reading of
the line as "a bill of rights on managed care and flirting." And in
the following sentence:

> I announced to Rogers that I had examined his
> records and called the auditors.

Again a comma may be needed to prevent ambiguity. If I told
Rogers that I had both examined the records and called the
auditors, no punctuation is necessary, as "called the auditors" is
not an independent sentence. However, if the meaning of the
sentence is that I first told Rogers, then called the auditors, a
comma after records is necessary and justified:

> I announced to Rogers that I had examined his
> records, and called the auditors.

That should honestly do it. If you stick with these reasons to use commas, you'll most likely blow through in style. Reasons *not* to insert a comma include sensing a pause in mid-sentence (the ill-considered "breath comma") or simply a long sentence (the worse-considered "death comma"— death, that is, to your image as a writer in control).

☞ The colon (:)

A colon serves two principal functions:

1. To open a business letter.

   Dear John:

2. To indicate that an explanation, a list, or fuller detail follows. It's like a more formal dash.

   Mr. Pritzer, the current CEO, named three objectives: to make money, to expand operations, and to restore the firm's good name.

   There's no need to restrict coverage by price: consultants should continue to offer both low-cost and high-cost plans.

   For example: (1) the lifetime maximum plan; (2) the daily maximum plan; and (3) the modified comprehensive plan

Note: Avoid interrupting running copy (sentences in paragraphs) with a colon. That means do *not* use it like a little trumpet, ta da, in the middle of your sentence:

> No: I'd like everyone to bring: a monthly work update, a calendar, and a tentative schedule for next month.

Try to complete your sentence before you insert the colon (as I did this one):

> Yes: I'd like everyone to bring the following items: a calendar...

> Yes: I'd like everyone to bring a calendar...

☞ The dash (—)(–)

The em dash (the longest one) is used to

1. express a sharp break in thought:

> But to embezzle from the poorest of her clients—can you believe it?

2. introduce detail about foregoing material, like a less

formal colon:

> We've identified three possible locations for the
> headquarters—Chicago, Atlanta, and Durham.

3. add information that might also be bracketed by
commas or parentheses, as in this example:

> The building was slated to be demolished—on
> May 15, in fact—when an offer came in from
> Whitman in Los Angeles.

When using dashes in this way, be sure you remember to put them in pairs:

> No: She turned away—she obviously didn't want
>   to speak and made her way to a side exit.

> Yes: She turned away—she obviously didn't want
>   to speak—and made her way to the side exit.

The en dash (–) is half the length of the em dash in
printing. It indicates a range of numbers, dates,
times, or the like: 1—100, January 20—25, 9:00—
5:00 p.m.

☞ **The hyphen (-)**

I've said punctuation helps clarify meaning. Many people
don't understand the principle of hyphenation, but hyphens
exist for very specific purpose: they help show the relationships
between words. Consider these two sentence, for example (art-
fully contrived solely to prove my point):

> The customer ordered twenty three quarter inch
> sheets of plywood.
>
> Please deliver ninety-five hundred dollar bills.

Where you put the hyphen or hyphens matters a lot. In the
first sentence, as you can see, *twenty-three sheets*, each *a quarter of
an inch* thick, is quite different from *twenty sheets*, each *three-
quarters of an inch* thick. Depending on where you put the
hyphens, you'll get a satisfied customer or a displeased and puz-
zled one. In the second, is it ninety-five bills, each worth one
hundred dollars? or ninety-five hundred bills worth one dollar
each? The delivery man wants to know whether to ride his bike
or get out the truck. Here's how to hyphenate in each case:

> …ninety-five hundred-dollar bills
>
> …ninety-five hundred dollar bills

In the following headline and church bulletin item, which
are grammar-industry classics, one missing hyphen in each case

has created a major confusion of meaning:

Squad Helps Dog Bite Victim

The ladies of the church have cast off clothing of
every kind in the parish basement

While such faux pas may be highly amusing, especially to
collectors of same in communications, bear in mind that your
boss may not be amused to find them in your writing.

Here are a very few principles that will cover the greater
part of hyphen usage:

1. Use your dictionary. It lists an amazing number of
   compounds—*hyphenated*: long-term, self-righteous,
   one-half; *closed position*: longtime, firsthand, reorder,
   multinational, workforce; *open position*: growth
   industry, circuit board, cross section (as a noun).

2. Use a hyphen **to join a descriptive pair or series of
   words preceding the noun** they describe. These are
   usually temporary constructions and the form is
   very familiar:

   tax-deductible interest, fast-paced presentation

There's a reason for this. Take the phrase "odd looking glass," for example. Is it a looking glass that's odd? or a glass that is odd looking? "Top flight industry," "level premium method," and "fast moving truck" belong in the same category. The convention of hyphenating says that leaving them open (unhyphenated) means the last two words are described by the first; hyphenating the first two leaves no doubt they are a pair describing the third.

However, when the descriptive words *follow* the noun they modify, there's little chance of confusion:

the interest is tax deductible

the presentation seemed fast paced

When using very familiar pairs of words such as *nursing home* or *interest rate* as descriptive phrases, though it's not incorrect to use one, you don't need the hyphen: nursing home costs, interest rate hikes.

3. There's an exception to Rule 2: **you need not hyphenate after -*ly* adverbs**, such as *chemically, wholly, attractively*, nor the familiar adverb *very*. Because their appearance indicates their function in the sentence, confusion is unlikely.

a wholly owned subsidiary; a clearly advantageous

strategy; a very good idea

Again, I'm hitting high spots. These principles will get you most of the way. In the unlikely event that you want more, the last time I looked *The Chicago Manual of Style* had eleven pages devoted to the proper use of hyphens. Enjoy.

☞ **The apostrophe (')**

This isn't hard. Yet since people get their knickers in a twist about it, we might as well get it right the first time. The apostrophe is used to indicate two scenarios:

1. Possession:

SINGLE NOUN OR NAME	POSSESSIVE: ADD ('S)
company	company's
Joan	Joan's
Business	business's
Charles	Charles's

Now you have two minutes to ventilate and complain that you learned in school to drop the final *s* after a single noun ending in *s*. Some people did teach that, and some learned it. As for me and virtually all the reputable style manuals, we don't give you even the option. Why? because this form is less likely to be misunderstood. And because it is what most people actually say when they pronounce a possessive. Try pronouncing it. "Lewis's fund." As opposed to, say, "the Lewis Fund."

Exceptions: Ancient Greek and Biblical names, such as Achilles and Moses, and for *goodness'* or *conscience' sake.*

Some people complain that the rule results in some unwieldy constructions, such as "Massachusetts's industry." All right, but assuming you have more resources than dumb driven cattle, you can simply write around it: "The industry of Massachusetts" or simply "Massachusetts industry" (like "U.S. industry") is accurate and euphonious. A woman named Alexis in one of my seminars told us her fourth-grade teacher had been unequivocal about the possessive of her name, *'s*: it was "*Alexis's* boots," not *Alexis'.* I could tell the class was more impressed by this story than by anything I'd said on the subject.

PLURAL NOUN ENDING IN S	ADD (')
businesses	businesses'
professors	professors'
taxes	taxes'
Joneses (Mr. and Mrs. together)	Joneses'

PLURAL NOUN NOT ENDING IN S	ADD ('S)
women	women's
people	people's
courts-martial	courts-martial's
alumni	alumni's

If the apostrophe denotes possession, in referring to a company's balance sheet, why do we say *its*, rather than *it's*, balance sheet? We looked at this in Chapter 12 on pronouns—it's because all the pronouns, being a zillion years old, do their own thing. They're irregular and *never* take a possessive apostrophe. That's right, never. It's comforting. Write *his*, *hers*, *yours*, *its*, *ours*, *theirs*, *whose*.

2. Omission An apostrophe can also mean a letter has been left out:

I can't, she didn't, I'm, they're, it's (for *it is* or *it has*), the '90s

Be sure to put the apostrophe where the missing letter would have gone. If you have trouble with this, spell checkers are very clear about it, which leaves no excuse for writing *does'nt* or *its'*.

The convention of using *'s* to indicate the plural of abbreviations and numbers—*the 1940's*, *ABC's*—is like the lava lamp: retro, a little weird, not for serious use. It's too easily mistaken for a possessive. Write simply

Local YMCAs, ATMs, the 1990s, the '80s

Exceptions: if your abbreviation contains more than one period, if it ends in an *s*, or if a simple *s* could otherwise cause confusion, add *'s*:

She holds two *M.A.'s* from the University of Michigan.

Her memos usually represent *SOS's*.

The new interns are minding their *p's* and *q's*.

☞ The period (.)

Note in the examples above that most of the abbreviations are without periods, or points, a convention that's becoming increasingly familiar:

NYSE, ROI, CIA, CD ROM, NAACP, IMF

If your organization prefers to use points/periods with certain acronyms or abbreviations, that's fine: just be sure you communicate this to everyone writing for you and are consistent in your treatment, especially within a piece. If you are writing to an organization that abbreviates its name, do exactly as the organization does, no matter what your house style.

Time out: why did I write "acronyms or abbreviations"? What's the difference? Thank you for asking. An acronym is a word you can pronounce—*NATO, radar, NOW*—formed from the initial letters of a name or a series of words. A *WAC* is a member of the Women's Army Corps. *Snafu* stands for Situation Normal: All Fouled Up (Wait—you heard the "f" stood for what?) An abbreviation may be either an acronym or simply the shortened form of a word: *gal.* for *gallon, etc.* for *et cetera,* Vt. for Vermont.

Back to work. Periods end sentences and go *inside* quotation marks. You do not need them after items in a vertical list unless one or more items are complete sentences:

> In case of fire, follow these steps:
> - Dial 911 to report the fire.
> - Use stairways, not elevators.
> - Leave the building and remain outside.

> The Royal 500 has three modes
> - Ready
> - Standby
> - Power saver

☞ Quotation marks (" ")

1. Use quotation marks to enclose someone's exact words:

> Your client then asked me, "Why on earth should I pay Henry?"

2. Use them to introduce an unfamiliar word or phrase:

"To indemnify" means to protect against damage,
loss, or injury.

3. Use them to indicate that something is so-called but
phony:

He offered us a chance to get in on a "sure thing."

The inference in that sentence is that the horse,
stock, or whatever is anything *but* sure.

People sometimes have trouble remembering whether to put
punctuation inside or outside quotation marks. The problem is
complicated if you read books printed in Great Britain, where
the marks go inside or outside, depending on whether they are
part of the quoted material or not. For Americans, the system is
illogical but easy: remember that no matter what logic indicates,
quotation marks always go outside periods and commas;
otherwise, they go inside or out according to whether the colon,
semicolon, question mark, or whatever is part of the quoted
material:

His idea of a "revolving bond fund," quoted in the
article "Narrow Rate Spreads," might have been
viable when interest rates were high, but I feel it
is poorly suited to today's financial environment.

Why did you quote his article, "Narrow Rate Spreads"? I have investigated the concept of a "revolving bond fund": it offers no potential for our market today.

Why do periods and commas always go inside quotation marks? A story, possibly apocryphal, explains why and may help you remember where they belong. Before the invention of automatic typesetting, printers discovered that if they set type with a quotation mark followed by a period or a comma, like this— (".) —these very small punctuation marks often got knocked off the end of the line of type. Accordingly, they began putting the periods and commas safely *in*side the quotation marks, where they remain to this day.

Don't overuse quotation marks. You may enclose an unfamiliar word or phrase in quotation marks the first time you use it. Once you've identified or explained it, however, you don't need to keep wrapping the quotation marks around it. In fact, you shouldn't, because it's distracting and a little annoying.

Speaking of which, I don't think you'd do this, but just in case you're tempted, don't ever use quotation marks, in advertising or elsewhere, to highlight a name or description:

Jayne's Homemade "Ice Cream"

Visit Dale's showroom and get the "best rates around"!

Although you may be using them as an attention-getting

device, like boldface type, it looks entirely too much as if you're using them in the sense of (3) above. As though Jayne is, in fact, making ice cream out of recycled Styrofoam and Dale has lousy rates. I drove past a mailbox once that said "The Holtons": my family and I made rude remarks about who actually could be living there under the alias of Holton. Amelia Earhart? Jimmy Hoffa? Apparently not the Holtons.

☞ Single quotation marks (' ')

Some people use these, for no good reason, in place of the double marks. Please don't: they have a very specific function. They serve to enclose another quotation, or a title that would ordinarily be enclosed in quotation marks, within quoted material. Here's an example:

> Mr. Forbes said, "Your article, "Getting Rich on a
> Fixed Income," strained the credibility of the
> *Forbes* editorial board."

In business writing you're probably not going to need single quotation marks often.

☞ The semicolon (;)

Two very useful functions performed by the semicolon are

1. To connect two complete sentences that are related in thought. You may include a conjunction such as

and or *but*, but it's not necessary, as it is when a comma is the joining mark:

I don't blame you for asking to see the man's identification; he doesn't look like one of our regular couriers.

We can take the taxi to the airport early in the afternoon; but I've been wondering if the train wouldn't be a better idea.

The semicolon makes a break sharper than that of the comma, but not so sharp as that of a period.

2. To divide and clarify a series that contains internal punctuation. The semicolon is an excellent device to avoid confusion in such cases. For example, here's a sentence with a structure particularly familiar from photo captions:

Key members of the systems team are shown above. They are, from left, John Erskine, first vice president with overall responsibility for coordinating the effort company-wide, Mary Jane Abdul, systems designer, Susan Atkins, our team leader, Ann Brownell, administrative assistant, and Harry Hartwell, head programmer.

If you're reading carefully, you can match names and functions. It's easy in a casual reading, however, to read "our team leader, Ann Brownell," and so on. To ensure that descriptive information attaches clearly to the person intended, the semicolon functions as a sort of firewall, dividing more strongly than the commas:

> John Erskine, first vice president with overall responsibility for coordinating the effort company-wide; Mary Jane Abdul, systems designer; Susan Atkins, our team leader; Ann Brownell, administrative assistant; and Harry Hartwell, head programmer.

☞ Slash (/)

This mark, also known as a virgule, can join two words or phrases with the useful meaning of *this*, *that*, or *both*:

> Jack Davis functions as our plant manager/purchasing agent.

Evidently, since the two functions are not readily blended, Jack operates sometimes as plant manager, sometimes as purchasing agent, and, presumably on bad days, as both. That's a good use for the slash. Don't start slashing around, however; you can overwork this mark by using it as a substitute for a hyphen or the word "and":

> Ilene Farber was named president/CEO of Aitken
> Industries in May.

Remember that the slash adds that interesting suggestion of *or*. Ilene isn't president *or* CEO, she's both. So say *president-CEO* or *president and CEO*.

The slash is used perhaps most often in the construction *and/or*. Here's a legitimate use for this one, where either or both is meant:

> As time permits, please show our prospect the
> Data Automation building, the new paint room,
> and/or the automated punch press operation.

Don't get crazy with *and/or* either: it gets to be a distracting tic in some people's writing. Possibly they think it covers all contingencies and therefore captures some sort of quasi-legal high ground. Actually, it's more often simply tedious. Ask yourself whether *and* or *or* alone wouldn't be simpler and just as accurate:

> Please bring a copy of your most recent paystub,
> mortgage statement, and/or IRS records for the
> preceding year.

Come on. Will it really improve the situation if this poor soul goes and digs out all three? Write *or*.

☞ **Parentheses (( ))**

Try not to use these if you don't have to. They break up your line visually, and they tend to imply the information is unimportant. Commas work better for material that's closely related to the rest of the sentence:

> No: Our chairman and CEO (Francis Brownell)
> resigned today.

> Yes: Our chairman and CEO, Francis Brownell,
> resigned today.

Punctuate and capitalize with parentheses like this:

> At Feradyne (not to be confused with Teradyne),
> we do only finish work.

> I learned double-entry bookkeeping last fall (it
> isn't hard).

> We asked him to give an overview of the proposed
> system. (He had volunteered to provide one at his
> expense.)

Don't place punctuation ahead of a phrase in parentheses:

> No: When I arrive, (assuming the plane's on time)

I'll go straight to Belcorp.

Yes: When I arrive (assuming the plane's on time),
        I'll go…

Yes: We arrived. (The plane was on time.) We
        went…

☞ Brackets ([ ])

Like the single quotation marks, brackets are second-generation parentheses: that is, they go inside a pair of parentheses if you must excerpt something within the parenthesized material:

Gauchand-Eiger (whose largest plant [see map of
facilities, page 14] is in Lausanne) is a major
target for takeover by our Swiss subsidiary.

Brackets are also useful if you must interject a comment of your own when quoting someone else's writing or speech:

Gleasman's comments on the Web site follow: The
printouts of the Web site have two parts. As the
site was designed to be shown on screen [as part
of the Olympic demo], some printouts appear to
have text missing.

The word *sic*, Latin for *thus*, means that's the way the person you're quoting wrote or said it. Sort of a mean way of pointing out an error while noting it's not of your doing. It is generally italicized and bracketed:

> This is in fact whitetext [*sic*] that will not appear
> in printouts.

☞ Exclamation point (!)

Even if you're writing advertising copy, I recommend limiting the use of this mark. Heavily exclamatory writing makes you appear unsophisticated and perhaps overly excitable. Calvin Trillin says it's a bad way of calling attention to your line, like laughing at your own joke. Indeed.

The mark (?!) is one I feel sure you'll never need, but I cherish it as a reminder of my comic-book-reading days. In case you're interested, printers call it an **interrobang**.

Punctuation marks are little, but don't think for a minute they're unimportant. They function like street signs along an unfamiliar route: by clarifying meaning and explaining the function of sentence elements, they help your readers remain on course as they negotiate the hills, turns, and straightaways of your prose.

—— THE BOTTOM LINE ——

- **Use this chapter as your guide to selecting and using punctuation correctly.**

CHAPTER 19

HAVE I CHOSEN CONCRETE LANGUAGE WHENEVER POSSIBLE?

Don't overuse abstract words. Convenient as they are, they have a big downside. I'm talking about such words as these:

facility	circumstance
performance	relationship
contact	impact
event	equipment
effect	situation
function	result

Navigating the business world, you may have noted a disquieting preference for the general-category or all-purpose word rather than the specific one. What a quick and easy way to drain your writing of color and make it forgettable! What's the reason for this peculiar preference? It may reflect caution, a refusal to get specific and risk one's backside. Or perhaps it's a (faulty) perception that these words are, by their very lack of color, businesslike. Whatever the cause, it's unattractive and it's information poor. Consider the following sentences:

>   Please *contact* me if you have any questions.

>   We plan to break ground for the new *facility* in May.

Then compare the punch delivered by

>   Please *call me at 203-872-8448* if you have any questions.

>   We plan to break ground for the new *modern art museum* in May.

In a few words, that's the difference between concrete and what I call "covering" language.

Contact and *facility* are examples of covering language. There's no denying such words are useful, because just one will cover a number of possibilities. You can *contact* someone, for example, by many methods: phone, fax, e-mail, and carrier pigeon, to name but a few. And *facility* can describe a multiplex of buildings and structures, from offices to warehouses to lighthouses to phone booths and portable lavatories.

But because they apply in a range of situations, covering words are by nature imprecisely focused. They are abstractions that create little or no visual impression, and therefore they are not memorable. And you are not supposed to substitute them for concrete, specific words. People do it anyhow, I'm sorry to say. Sometimes they even write "Please *contact* me at 631-7967 if you have any questions." This is not what covering words were designed for.

A covering word such as *event* allows us to describe things that may be dissimilar but that occupy the same position relative to the sense of a sentence. A covering word such as *events* is practically indispensable to describe the disparate items listed below:

> Research indicates that a job change, the birth or
> death of a child, and a change in health are major
> *events* that can threaten a marriage.

But I would never, ever, *ever* use the word *event* as a substitute for *marathon*, or *ribbon cutting*, or *cocktail party*, any more than I would describe a *marriage* as a *relationship*:

> The Jewetts are holding an event at the Ritz to
> commemorate their relationship.

That kind of writing raises more questions than it answers. Focus as sharply as possible on the specifics and be memorable:

> The Jewetts are celebrating their 30th wedding
> anniversary with an all-night black-tie dinner
> dance for 200 people at the Ritz.

If the newspaper mentions the possibility of a "precipitation event," do you get a mental picture of what's going to happen? Now if the weatherfolk are considering the possibility of everything from cats and dogs to lemon drops falling from the sky, there's justification for *precipitation*, if not *event*: the word covers a number of conditions. But I'd always prefer to read *rain, snow, sleet*, or *hail*. Not to mention lemon drops. How different and specific are the feelings each of those words evokes! We're creatures of matter and space ourselves, after all, not bodiless abstractions. We yearn for words that engage our senses.

(Same issue, different context: I hate it when a new bride thanks me for my "gift" without naming it specifically. She can't identify a casserole dish? The groom could be in for some bad surprises.)

Even harder on your readers is covering language that yields no clue to the nature of what it's supposed to describe. It covers so many possibilities that it is "spineless": you can't tell whether you're reading good or bad news. For example:

> The new regulation will have a profound *impact* on
> our revenues.

Impact, my foot. Evidently, somebody stands to make or lose a lot of money. I can think of no reason why the writer should keep readers in the dark as to which. Take your pick:

> The new regulation will *triple* our revenues.

> The new regulation will *devastate* our revenues.

Now that's news you can sink your teeth into. That's good, because business writing is starved for specifics. Whenever it's at all possible, turn those covering words loose in favor of concrete ones. If several different options are possible and you want to leave them all open, then go with covering language. But if you can hone in sharply, you'll create an image in a reader's mind that will linger, prompting, with any luck, the response you want.

Preferring the concrete word may give you another, subliminal advantage. Author and former news commentator Robert MacNeil, now chairman of the MacDowell Colony, makes an intriguing point in his autobiography, *Wordstruck*. Most of the abstract words in our language are derivatives of Latin, which, dating from the arrival of Christianity in England at the end of the sixth century, was the language of the church, of thought and knowledge, and of the upper classes. As such, words borrowed from Latin tend to represent abstract concepts. They also tend to be long, because you know the Romans: they took a root, added a bunch of prefixes and suffixes, and voila! *contradistinctively*.

The words derived from Old English, on the other hand, can tell them from the Latin derivatives because they are Anglo-Saxon monosyllables: mostly short. These words are the language of the concrete: the words for food and shelter, family, the human body. *Mother, father, head, hand, foot, bread, meat, milk, love, home, heart.* These are the words for our basic needs, and they constitute a child's earliest vocabulary, notes MacNeil. He theorizes that when you use these words, you reach people at an emotional as much as a rational level. You make a subliminal appeal to them. That can't be bad for business.

Well, yes, but how can we really pull that off in business writing? By valuing the short word as much as the long one.

Just because a word is long doesn't make it impressive: *help* is every bit as good a word as *facilitate*. Also, you just might score subliminal points by putting in a word derived, I mean *gotten*, from Old English when you get the chance:

> Rogene Systems is the data processing *arm* of the company.

I'm not being frivolous: try it. It certainly can't hurt. And if you check the supreme stylists of the English language—from William "To Be Or Not To Be" Shakespeare to E.B. "Some Pig" White—you're going to be forced to admit that for them, the Anglo-Saxon monosyllables are the words of choice.

—— THE BOTTOM LINE ——

- **Use concrete, specific language whenever you can.**

- **Use covering, abstract language to refer to elements that differ or are unknown.**

CHAPTER 20

HAVE I BEEN AMBIGUOUS, ILLOGICAL, OR OFF THE WALL?

One of the most important aspects of business is gaining the confidence of clients, customers, and colleagues. You don't want to erode their confidence by making what I call "What th—?" statements—statements that would have caused an old-time comic book hero to utter that scrupulously clean 1950s expletive. Take this sentence, for example, recently gleaned from the front page of my morning paper:

> Funds to renovate the overcrowded, rundown
> building are expected to die Wednesday in the
> Legislature.

Incoming! Dead funds in the halls of Congress! I'm guessing that for lack of space the original caption, which probably began with "A proposal to fund" or "A bill for funding," was shortened, with fatal results. Bills dying we're used to; not funds. You can't afford this kind of careless writing if you want to impress readers.

That caption unimpressed me intensely, and my opinion of the newspaper, never high, fell another few points.

Here's how to purge your writing of ambiguous, illogical, and off-the-wall declarations that can hurt you and your organization.

☞ **Make pronoun references clear.** Your readers need to know, without having to dig around for it, to what or whom a pronoun refers. In the sentence below, meaning and communication aren't well served because it's impossible to tell whether *she* and *her* refer to Rachel or Anne:

> Originally, Rachel and Anne were scheduled to work together, but when *she* became ill, *she* turned over *her* responsibilities to Ken.

There are at least three possible ways to read the sentence. That's no kindness to the reader. Try

> Originally, Rachel and Anne were scheduled to work together, but when *Anne* became ill, *Rachel* turned over *Anne*'s responsibilities…

I'll grant you it isn't elegant, but the meaning is clear. In context you may be able to put it more gracefully:

> Originally, the two colleagues were scheduled to

work together, but when *Rachel* became ill, *Anne* turned over *her manager's...*

Also, be sure your pronouns refer to an actual name or noun, not to some hazy but unexpressed concept. Look at the following sentence:

> Marshall said he could construct a new stone wall for Regis Corp., but he wouldn't design the building facade: *it* was too difficult for him.

What was too difficult? You cannot point, as you must be able to, to a specific noun for which *it* stands in the sentence. That's because the pronoun refers to nothing solid or explicitly named in the sentence, but, apparently, to the effort to design the facade, or the design, or the creation of the design. In the revision below, *it* clearly stands for the noun *design*:

> ...but he wouldn't attempt *the design* of the building facade: *it* was too difficult for him.

☞ **Avoid incoherent noun references as well.**

> Ms. Keyser operates a 15-million-gallon ethanol plant, an industry that appears to have a bright future.

> The new *product*, a petroleum additive, is our *goal*
> for this quarter.

Fuel production is an industry—an ethanol plant is not. And a product rollout by mid-February may be a goal, but calling a product a goal is vague and illogical.

☞ **Be sure your comparisons are matching and finished off.** The wheeze about comparing apples to oranges applies importantly in writing. This, for example, is an incoherent comparison:

> My *job* is more difficult than my *manager*.

Although your manager may indeed be difficult, the items you compare have to match, so in that sentence you must compare job with job. Write *my manager's*, *my manager's job*, or *that of my manager*. The same applies in the following sentence:

> Our *GNP* is twice as big as *Japan*.

No, actually it isn't. It's twice as big as *Japan's GNP*. Be sure you're comparing apples to apples.

Your comparisons must also be finished. Here is a sentence containing two comparisons, only one of which is complete:

> The new salesman is *as good* or *better than* his
> predecessor.

Though I hate to keep saying this, you can't say that. There's
no problem with *better than his predecessor*. But *as good his prede-*
cessor? *as good than his predecessor*? The comparison is incom-
plete, because it's missing a word:

> The new salesman is as good *as* or better than his
> predecessor.

Finally, don't write a comparative word such as *better* or *further*
without saying, if at all possible, better or further than *what*. I know
advertising makes lavish use of this device: the airlines fly you farther, the new bleach gets your wash whiter, and it's better in the
Bahamas. But in the overwhelming majority of cases, you should
complete the comparison, for the sake of coherence and clarity:

> No: Our company offers better benefits.

> Yes: Our company offers better benefits *than the*
> *company that has made you an offer.*

> No: Harry's presentation was more convincing.

> Yes: Harry's presentation was more convincing
> *than Lee's.*

Don't forget that you as the writer *know* than what or whom; the person to whom you're writing may know; another person who reads your work may very well have no idea. Don't chance it. Besides, finished comparisons just sound better. I mean better than unfinished ones.

☞ **Put modifying phrases near their subject.** A descriptive phrase tends to attach itself to whatever is closest to it. Consider these two sentences:

> Reynolds suggested that we merge our two companies over cocktails.

> Susan will move into the cubicle next to the refrigerator, which was my original office.

In the first, the phrase *over cocktails* appears to refer to the proposed merger, putting a peculiar slant on the whole idea. In fact, the phrase properly belongs to *Reynolds suggested* and should be placed accordingly. In the second, *which was my original office* suggests by its placement that our writer previously occupied office space in the refrigerator. A slight rewrite will prevent this embarrassing misperception:

> *Over cocktails*, Reynolds suggested that we merge our two companies.

> Susan will move into *my original office*, the cubicle
> next to the refrigerator.

☞ **Don't mix metaphors.** An alert friend called to report this awe-inspiring gaffe made by a Virginia senator on national television:

> My colleague is leading you through a Byzantine
> thicket of quicksand.

A mixed metaphor is a pileup of two, or in this case three, figures of speech on one another. Byzantine means intricate, often bejeweled. Thickets aren't Byzantine, and they aren't made of quicksand, either. Such bloopers give the impression that a writer is at least partially out of control. Here's another:

> The ship of state is leaping the hurdles of foreign
> tariffs.

Ships don't leap hurdles. Runners leap hurdles, and the twain shouldn't be meeting in that sentence. And I'm horrified that the following is the work of a school principal:

> The principal is a one-man band who puts out
> fires and maintains his sacred cows.

By all means use metaphors in your writing: business writing in particular is desperate for color. But be careful of such unintended mixing: it may be entertaining, but it makes readers question your reliability, if not your sanity.

☞ **Don't dangle participles or modifiers.** The names may sound intimidating, but these are relatively easy to deal with. If you don't deal with them, dangling participles and dangling modifiers can also produce perhaps the most spectacular "what th—"s in the writing business. Here are three examples:

> Sputtering, popping, and blowing fuses, the marketing director helplessly watched his presentation self-destruct in the antiquated projector.

> In day care since the age of two, his parents were prominent attorneys.

> Having spent an exciting weekend in Los Angeles, my briefcase was missing.

Though in principle I have nothing against marketing heads popping fuses, parents languishing in day care, and briefcases on weekend escapades, such errors make your writing look less than serious. And writing that's hard to take seriously is not good business writing. These amazing effects are achieved, once again, through location: the modifier, beginning with an *-ing* word if it's a participial phrase, attaches itself to the very first noun it encounters. If that noun is not the real subject of the descriptive phrase, you have a problem—as you can see from the examples above. You have two options for grounding these dangling constructions: (1) Be sure the *real* subject of the phrase is the next noun *after* the comma:

> Sputtering, popping, and blowing fuses, *the antiquated projector* destroyed the marketing director's presentation.

Or (2) make sure the subject is expressed in the phrase itself, *preceding* the comma:

> As *the antiquated projector* began sputtering, popping, and blowing fuses, the marketing director helplessly watched it destroy his presentation.
>
> 1. In day care since the age of two, *he* was the son of two prominent attorneys.
>
> 2. *He* had been in day care since the age of two; his parents were prominent attorneys.
>
> 1. Having spent an exciting weekend in Los Angeles, I discovered my briefcase was missing.
>
> 2. After *I* had spent an exciting weekend in Los Angeles, my briefcase…

In the following sentence, the meaning's so clear it may be hard to spot the problem:

> Reviewing your proposal this morning, everything
> has gone wrong.

But the problem exists, and the sentence is as off as a bad egg. *Everything* can't review proposals. To eliminate the dangling participle, you must say something along these lines:

> 1. Reviewing your proposal this morning, *I* have
> had a series of mishaps.

> 2. *I* have been trying to review your proposal this
> morning, but everything has gone wrong.

☞ **Edit out "no-way" statements.** Finally, don't give readers a reason to respond "No way!" when they read your stuff. It's easy to make no-way statements—if you're writing hastily, editing carelessly, or simply too close to your material. It's hard to believe it, but the following three sentences are the work, respectively, of a magazine reporter, a columnist for a major daily, and an advertising copywriter for a large corporation:

> The early years of the magazine were an exciting
> place to work.

The fiddlehead ferns are past being edible to pick.

Sometimes a once-in-a-lifetime opportunity comes along.

My daughter Sarah, at age 10 a discerning little soul, read that last one over my shoulder and denounced as "weird" the notion that a once-in-a-lifetime event could happen *sometimes*—once a month, maybe?

It's kind of funny when someone else does it—but just one of these statements can undermine a reader's confidence in you. Read carefully before you print or send to be sure you haven't said something impossible or ridiculous.

——— THE BOTTOM LINE ———

- **Be sure your pronouns refer clearly to their subjects.**

- **Watch incoherent references: a product is not a goal.**

- **Compare similar items; complete your comparisons.**

- **Put descriptive phrases near their subjects.**

- **Don't mix metaphors.**

- **Don't dangle participles or modifiers.**

- **Never give your reader cause to say "No way!"**

CHAPTER 21

HAVE I SWEATED THE SMALL STUFF?

I know I've made this point frequently, but I'm guessing you need to hear it again: it's worth it to sweat the small stuff. Some of the people who read your work will be put off by even the littlest mistakes. In fact, some people evidently go looking for them. A Dilbert cartoon shows Wally returning Dilbert's report with "a few thousand suggestions" and the following comment: "Of all the pleasures of life, I think I like nit-picking the best." The small stuff is important because it's possible the people you want to impress are people like Wally. The following glitches are small ones indeed, but they can raise a disproportionate amount of complaint when they appear. If discriminating readers get the impression you're careless or ignorant in these small things, they are less likely to trust your message.

☞ **Don't overuse capital letters.** Observe four big rules for the use of capital letters:

1. **Capitalize the proper names** of persons, places, and things, as I hope Mrs. Adams taught you in fourth

grade (Dare I hope they're teaching *anything* about correct writing in these last days? The Grammar Goths are over the wall and confusion reigns).

2. **Look in a good style manual** such as *Chicago* or *Words into Type* to get the scoop on particular cases: governmental bodies, regions of the country, etc. Both will tell you to capitalize *Northeast* (sales in the Northeast) but not *government* (U.S. government), *English* but not *economics*, and so on.

3. **Observe house style.** Whether you use initial caps for certain words or categories of words—such as the titles of people or divisions in your organization—is to a certain extent a function of your company's style. If there is such a thing, written or unwritten, make yourself familiar with it and use it.

4. **Minimize.** Beyond the first three rules, I'd counsel you to lay the caps on very lightly. Overdone, they tend to make your writing look Victorian or even older. You don't want to be mistaken for a member of the Heaving Bosom School of Writing. Business writing shouldn't appear frenetic. Also, capitals distract by making your line stutter: the eye is forced up and down, up and down as you read. Here's an excerpt from the United States Constitution, drafted in 1787, that makes heavy use of initial caps:

Article. IV, Section 1: Full Faith and Credit shall be given in each State to the public Acts, Records, and judicial Proceedings of every other State.

So goes the entire document: it's like German, with practically every noun capitalized. To the modern American eye, it's odd, possibly even a little breathless. Compare that with an amendment to the same document, proclaimed in 1971:

Amendment XXVI: The right of citizens of the United States, who are 18 years of age or older, shall not be denied or abridged by the United States or any state on account of age.

Very easy on the eyes. What a difference 200 years makes! That's how it's typically done these days.

By the same token, though, easy on the eyes can translate into "doesn't catch one's attention." For this reason, especially if you're a writer of promotional copy, you probably make use of capital letters as well as font treatment, point size, and other techniques to draw your readers' attention and create emphasis:

Be sure to visit our store during our Grand Opening Sale!

That's fine, but, as I suggested in Chapter 8, be

moderate in your use of these techniques—just look at the excerpt from Article IV, above: everything emphasized adds up to nothing emphasized.

☞ **Put your words in their proper places.** In general, a word belongs as close as possible to the words with which it's associated. If you observe this maxim, you'll measurably improve the clarity of your writing. Here are four adverbs (words that tell how) that tend to wander when you're not watching closely:

1. **Only.** Many people are careless with *only*, and the results are unsatisfactory. To be sure you're putting it in its proper place, say to yourself, "What is it that's *only*?" A philosopher might say, "In what does the onliness inhere?" Take a look at this example:

   If you only need to write a few checks each week…

   What's *only* in this sentence? The word's misplaced, because it isn't a question of only *needing*, as opposed, say, to *wanting*. And it isn't only *to write*, as opposed to *to photograph*.
   The correct answer is, of course, only *a few checks*, as opposed, perhaps, to *a lot*:

If you need to write *only* a few checks each week…

You can change the meaning of some sentences, depending on where you place *only*:

She improved *only* her bookkeeping when her manager complained (she did nothing about her keyboard skills).

She improved her bookkeeping *only* when her manager complained (then, and not earlier).

Here's another:

The auditor *only* asked me once for those expense records.

Although the sentence as written focuses attention on the act of asking, it seems clear from the context that the auditor asked *only once*.

2. **Just.** A similar issue. Be sure you place *just* as close as possible to what it modifies. Suppose you need three contracts to fund your payroll:

No: If we could *just* get three contracts, we could
meet payroll.

Yes: If we could get *just* three contracts, we could
meet payroll.

The emphasis belongs on the number, not the act
of getting. Compare with the following sentence, in
which the emphasis *is* on the act of getting:

If we could *just* get this contract, we could meet
payroll.

3. **Even.**

No: You are asked not to even touch one of the
buttons on the keypad.

Yes: You are asked not to touch even one of the
buttons....

It's clear this is not about touching, as opposed to,
say, bashing. Avoid splitting an infinitive as you zero
in on *one*, the real focus of the sentence.

4. **Almost.**

> No: I *almost* contacted every one of the marketing
>   reps.

> Yes: I contacted *almost* every one of the marketing
>   reps.

We're creatures of mind and spirit, but we are limited by physical space. And these spatial constraints offer an opportunity to home in very precisely on elements of meaning in our writing. Take advantage of them.

☞ **Treat abbreviations and acronyms correctly.** First, *identify* abbreviations unless they are as universally understood as, for example, MD or U.S. I recommend in most cases giving the full name first, then the abbreviated form in parentheses:

> The Americans with Disabilities Act (ADA)

> The Division of Youth Services (DYS)

You may then continue to use the abbreviation or acronym as you wish without further identification. You don't have to, of course: you may use the spelled-out version if for whatever reason you prefer it at a particular spot.

I need to get up on my orange crate to make my next pronouncement: I hope you can all hear me. Just because you express an abbreviation in capital letters does not necessarily mean that the word or phrase should be capitalized:

> Operational efficiencies are a feature of point-of-sale (POS) terminals.

> We expect to realize a stunning return on investment (ROI) through the merger.

Confusion sometimes arises over whether to put "a" or "an" before an abbreviation. You'll get it right every time if you say the article and the abbreviation aloud. For example:

> Please call Marjorie to find out whether we have *an* SBANE (pronounced *ess-bane*) meeting.

> We asked you for *a* SWIFT (pronounced *swift*) transmission.

> This is not *an* FDIC-insured (*eff-dee-eye-cee*) loan.

> *A* HIPAA (*hippa*) regulation prevents me from answering your question about the patient.

As I said in Chapter 18 on punctuation, the tendency nowadays is to write abbreviations without periods. Follow your organization's policy; if it's their abbreviation, follow theirs; follow your dictionary; if these guidelines are missing, be consistent in your own writing.

Write out United States as a noun in business copy, rather than using the abbreviations U.S. or USA. As a modifier, U.S. is fine: *the U.S. forces in Eastern Europe.*

A word about *versus*: In citing legal cases, the abbreviation for versus is written v.; in other uses, if you must abbreviate it—perhaps in a memo subject line—it's abbreviated *vs.*

Decades ago, in Roe v. Wade...

The advantages of the digital duplicator vs. the photocopier...

In everyday writing, I'd suggest you use *against*, or *as opposed to*, in preference to either.

☞ **Handle symbols with particular care.** Symbols that may be appropriate for certain other types of writing should not be used in business copy. In strictly mathematical or scientific copy, for example, the symbol % is used; in business copy, use the word *percent* unless you are going to be expressing pages and pages of percentages, as in, for example, an annual report.

Some symbols were used more commonly and with more justification when someone had to pull out an inkwell and a long piece of bird plumage in order to write. That's certainly the mood you create when you use them, and you should be aware of this. Such symbols include a favorite with some people (I have no idea why), the ampersand, or *&.* This mark is a substitute for the word *and*, and it is *so* over. It belongs in a letter from your three-times-great-grandfather that begins "Dear Wm" and signs off with "Yrs, Chas."

The ampersand is still used today in a couple of instances—in the names of firms: Callard & Bowser, Standard & Poor; R & D is a standard reference to research and development; and some agencies and businesses still use it when coining department or product names: Fisheries & Game Management, Marketing & Product Development, and the like. But please do not use an ampersand in place of "and" unless your marketing division has created a title or name that includes it (and if they haven't already printed up the letterhead stationery, stop them).

The same goes for #. This symbol for *number* may be used in scientific or mathematical writing, but it is not appropriate as a synonym for number in everyday business writing. Don't shame your organization by using the symbol this way:

> The # of people insisting on a refund is still very
> small.

I recently edited a letter for a young executive who referred several times to dollars, which he rendered as "$s." This would be fine if you were writing a note in haste to your spouse: "Stop at the ATM and get me some $s." It is not fine in your writing. Handle money respectfully.

☞ **Write out "don't use 'ems."** Like the infamous "no see'ums" of New England, tiny but infuriating biting insects, the "don't use 'ems" can ruin your day. Slap the following phrases into oblivion if you catch them in your work. A grab bag of baddies I've collected over time, these words and phrases may not always be incorrect, but they are considered poor usage by those who know. The reasons are various, complex, and mostly uninteresting, so I'm not going to wade into explaining. I'm just asking you as a favor to your readers, yourself, and me not to use them.

NOT	BUT
graduated school/college	graduated from school/college
I like/hate/prefer when like such and such	I like it when or, better, I
appreciate that you	appreciate your or appreciate it when you
same difference	it's all the same
different than	different from
did that already	has/have done that already
unlike in Detroit	unlike the Detroit meeting
unlike when you use a pen	unlike using a pen
as far as [whatever]	as far as [whatever] is concerned, or as for [whatever]

—— THE BOTTOM LINE ——

- Go easy on capital letters: less is more.

- Put words as close as possible to what they describe.

- Treat abbreviations and acronyms correctly.

- Handle such symbols as # and & cautiously, if at all.

- Edit a few phrases out of your writing permanently.

GETTING STARTED AND FOLLOWING THROUGH ON A WRITING PROJECT

Dorothy Parker supposedly once remarked, "Everyone wants to have written, but nobody wants to write." She knew what she was talking about. It's hard, sometimes excruciating. So much so that at least one writer, Colette, had to be locked in her room before she would actually settle down to the act of writing.

These writers are not alone. Many of us lesser literary lights are plagued by the fear of putting the words down on paper. Why? I'm reminded of a quotation from T.S. Eliot:

> Between the idea
> And the reality
> Between the motion
> And the act
> Falls the Shadow.

I've never known exactly what Eliot was talking about as far as his poem is concerned, but for me these words perfectly express the anxiety I feel before I write. I am so afraid that I won't be able to share my idea or argument in a form that will communicate. As grade school children sometimes tell their teachers, "I know the answer, I just can't find the words to say it." Teachers from time immemorial have riposted that if you know what you want to say you can so say it. But I think the children have a point. It can be so difficult it's sometimes almost threatening to try to find the right words. So difficult, in fact, that we back off from the very act of putting pen to paper or fingertips to keyboard. In fact so threatening that I quit writing this chapter right after the Eliot quotation and spent an hour prowling around the office to no profitable purpose.

Assuming then, that this is a common, not an abnormal, phenomenon, let's examine some strategies to make getting going on a piece of writing easier.

☞ **Limit your subject.** Don't take on more than you can handle. This means in every case restricting your own borders to some extent. More important, it means making sure what aspect of the subject the person who asked you to write about it had in mind. Be very sure you know what he or she wants you to target. Don't let anyone get away with handing you an unmanageable subject: both of you need to limit and clarify what's expected. Don't say, "Okay," for example, and dash off to do the job if someone asks you to write a report on temporary employees. The subject could fill the Astrodome. Are we talking about temps in your city? in the state? the United States? Well, let's assume the person meant the temporary employees in your company. What about them? Their numbers? their value to the company as compared to the permanent workforce? Their productivity? And so on. That's a broad example, obviously, but the point is that you and your manager need to be very sure you agree on exactly what it is you're meant to be tackling. Otherwise you may do a tremendous amount of work only to hear the dreaded words, "This isn't what I had in mind."

☞ **Be able to state your objective clearly. Be clear about your spin before you write.** Once you're clear on your topic, you can restrict it to the most important areas, rather than wandering off down paths that lead to no productive ends. What is your attitude toward your topic? Know beforehand whether you are going to recommend, blast, try to persuade. This will help guide your route through your piece of writing and accordingly lower your fear of what lies ahead in getting it down on paper.

☞ **Talk to yourself.** Get a dialogue going, if it doesn't make you feel silly and/or schizophrenic. Who knows? they might give you a private office with a real door if you talk to yourself a lot. Seriously, many experts advise getting this kind of conversation going as a prelude to writing. Ask yourself such questions as "Why am I writing this? What will convince my reader(s) that my argument is valid? What are the major points I must include? What's the logical order to put them in?" and so on. Oddly enough, this is not only useful, but it functions as a good stress-buster if you have a major load of anxiety about writing the piece.

☞ **Collect all the facts you need before you begin.**
Anxiety may begin or be heightened by the fact that deep inside, you *know* there's an important piece of information you need to complete your letter or report. Do *not* try to write around it or omit it. Sooner or later it's liable to trip you up. If there's a call you need to make, go ahead, even if you have to call Mr. Big a third time, talk your way past his assistant, and irritate them both. Leave the office, get in the car, drive back to the library. Get on the 'net and retrace your steps. It's worth it to know you have the facts and are in control of the piece, rather than the other way round.

☞ **Get what you want to say down in print.** Get it down in any form whatsoever. Think of the information you're loaded down with as a heavy weight: you need to get rid of it in any way you can. Just throw all the facts that are weighing you down on screen or even paper before you forget them. Don't worry if they seem disorganized. Get them down in print. Then you can stop worrying about them. It doesn't matter whether they make sense to anyone else or not: you know what you mean.

☞ **Consider an outline, however brief.** It sounds like grade school, I know, and nobody really likes to write an outline. I hate it, too. But I do it. Go ahead and jot one down. Don't worry about I, II, III, and A, 1, a, i. Just get the scheme down. It shows you one way to go. If you decide you don't want to go that way, the outline isn't in charge of you, you're in charge of it. Just change the outline.

One terrific thing an outline does for you is to help ensure an even depth of focus. Put itup on your Lucite stand or whatever and take a look from time to time as you write. If you've written down three points under the heading "Possible ways to increase sales in rural areas," you're less likely to spend your few precious hours going into minute detail on the first point at the expense of the other two.

☞ **Use a template.** Since we know reinventing the wheel isn't smart, and we're all tight on time, why not use a format that has worked in the past for you or someone else in your organization? You can take the bones, or structure, of a successful piece of writing, and infuse that form with your own data. It's not plagiarism, because you're not using the words, or even the ideas, of the other writer. Here are two letters, the template and the "copy":

I. Thank you for allowing me to talk with you about my qualifications for the position of retail operations analyst.

The opportunity to meet you and Ms. Kahn and to see how your company functions on a daily basis convinces me I'd be able to put my experience to good use at Savignac and Sons.

I enclose the transcript you requested as well as the names of two references. I look forward to hearing from you.

II. Thank you for participating in the recent focus group sponsored by Fenwick Mutual Life Insurance Company, which investigated why people select various insurance products.

The answers to the questionnaire you completed, as well as your thoughtful observations during the discussion, will help us serve all our customers better.

As a further way of expressing our thanks for your participation, I enclose two tickets to the opening of "Celebrities on Ice" at the City Center in March. We hope to see you there.

As you can see, the two letters have little in common—except their organization. The writer of II simply kept the organizational scheme of I and filled in the blanks. I can't take the space to show you here, but this can work equally well with a long report. Just be sure your original template is sound.

☞ **Consider the advantages of index or file cards.** It may sound strange, and it may bring back bad memories of school reports or worse. I merely said "consider." And there are a couple of advantages. For one thing, index cards allow you to manipulate your information physically in space. You have small bits of discrete data that can be moved around as necessary, and for those who are oriented toward the visual and the tactile, this can be extremely helpful. If you decide to remove some facts, out they come, but they can sit on a corner of your desk, readt to be reinserted should you change your mind. Also, as with the outline, if you plan to write about four equally important projects and see that your stack of cards about Project B is only half as high as that of Project D, you can see where your attention should be directed. All this is possible on a screen, at least in a sense, but it's not really the same.

If your piece of writing happens to be a speech, your index cards can move into the final phase with you—right into the conference room, boardroom, or auditorium. Cards work well in speeches because they quickly cue you, and you rarely lose your place, as can happen with a piece of paper.

If you use index cards, especially for a speech, here's one thing to remember: *be sure to number them* once you get them into their final sequence. I once debated an opponent who dropped her entire stack of cards. As people rushed to help her pick them up, the cards got hopelessly confused; so of course did she, and she lost the debate as a result (Although I endured some cheap humor afterward, my supporters did not in fact pick up her cards and shuffle them.)

☞ **Don't resort to delaying tactics.** Let's go about this procedure like adults. Looking up colorful quotations to include in your preface is nothing but procrastination in thin disguise. So is checking the thesaurus on your tool bar for synonyms. We've all done it: it's human nature. The problem with it is that it can literally waste hours that you should be spending writing. Yes, you do owe it to yourself to polish your product with these graceful touches—when you arrive at your final draft. Until then, leave blanks, underline poor word choices, write the next thing that comes into your head—do whatever you must to force the enterprise along. **Never try to write perfectly the first time through.** When you're writing your first draft, you're struggling to realize a shape, not burnishing the details.

☞ **Take a break. Take a break often.** The coffee break as a right for workers came in with Eleanor Roosevelt. Take advantage of your rights! Medical research shows coffee really does make you sharper, up to a point (the point at which you develop the capacity for self-sustained flight). But even more important than the caffeine, a break gives you perspective. If you get away from your work, you'll return to it refreshed and possibly even supplied with new insights. If you can combine a break with the benefits of oxygen, so much the better. Get outside if possible: go for a brisk walk or a run. The combination of removing yourself from the site of stress and distraction with the endorphins (read "happy hormones") exercise puts into the bloodstream, can produce a mental state of sometimes stunning clarity. I've found the solution to many writing problems, especially those involving organization of a report or arrangement of facts, along the three-mile neighborhood circuit I try to jog three times a week.

☞ **Don't stop when you're in trouble.** I said it's important to take breaks, but I have to highlight one critically important exception. Try never to leave a piece of writing when you've gotten lost. If you paint yourself into a corner where you sense the project has the wrong emphasis, or the writing needs to take a new direction, or it's just gotten so complicated you wonder whether you should throw it out and start over, it's a bad, bad time to take a break. Your reluctance to face the thing again will be tremendous. If this has ever happened to you, you know what I mean. You'll clean out your file cabinet before you'll look at that sucker again.

If you're badly stuck, don't walk out. It's far better to hang on until you see the place you want to be, albeit in the distance. Revise your outline. Underline the points you know you've got right. Take a few deep breaths. Then plunge right in again and keep after the copy till you've wrestled it into a shape you can live with. You can take a big break after that. When it's time to get back to work, you'll be glad you didn't quit while you were in trouble.

☞ **Visualize success.** Remind yourself how wonderful it feels, in Dorothy Parker's words, "to have written." Popular culture has been high on visualization techniques for a number of years. Borrowing from the trend, I try to visualize the current writing task getting smaller, and smaller, and finally vanishing altogether. And I recollect how utterly terrific I feel when I've completed a big writing assignment. Let yourself dwell on the feeling of relief and accomplishment of having completed a good piece of writing. Contrast it with the grim, gray, guilty way you feel when you have a piece hanging over you. Which feeling weighs more? Which do you prefer?

☞ **Let your deadline boost your adrenaline.** Samuel Johnson once said, "When a man knows he is to be hanged in a fortnight, it concentrates his mind wonderfully." For some people, a literal deadline has the same effect. But for them, two weeks ahead would be way too much time. They prefer to wait until the last minute, then ride the surge of adrenaline from start to finish. These are the people who chronically pulled all-nighters in college. If it works for you, go ahead. For someone my age, it's hard on the system. Besides, you never know: you might get flu or be called out of town. It takes faith to engage in serious procrastination. But you have to do what works for you.

NUMBERS: THE BASIC RULES

I t's almost impossible to play the numbers perfectly, because there are dozens of often-conflicting rules and an equally large number of exceptions. You've also got to take the nature of your organization into consideration: if it's a bank or an accounting firm, you may have very different requirements and constraints around the issue from, say, an outplacement bureau or a day care center. Let's try to inject some common sense into this area with a few generally accepted rules for use of numbers in business writing.

☞ **Write the numbers one through ten as words; for numbers 10 and up, use numerals.** This is the Number One Rule. You probably know it, and it works pretty well much of the time. If your organization prefers to write out one through twenty, or one through one hundred, that's fine, too. Maintain consistency within your organization if possible, and try to do the same within a piece of writing: that's the most important thing. And now that you're one with the rule, here come all the exceptions.

☞ **Express dates (month and year), street numbers, percentages, decimals, and numbered parts of a document (page, section, etc.) as numerals.** Even if they're below ten, these numbers are traditionally written as numbers, not words. Bet you knew this. Nobody writes "The real estate market had cooled off markedly by *two thousand and six.*"

> In 1978, in the 1970s, in the '70s
> 111 5th Street
> 3.14195265
> 8 percent
> page 22, section 4

☞ **In a series that mixes numbers above and below ten, choose one form.** If you want to advertise round-the-clock customer service, "24 hours a day, seven days a week," while it conforms to our Number One Rule, actually looks capricious and inconsistent. In such a case, either of these is appropriate:

> 24 hours a day, 7 days a week
> twenty-four hours a day, seven days a week

Let your graphic designer be your guide in choosing which form to use.

☞ **However, if you have numbers directly next to one another, you may want to express one as a numeral, the other as a word, to avoid confusion,** For example:

> No: I don't have enough small bills: I need at least *100 20s and 50 50s.*

> Yes: I don't have enough small bills: I need at least *100 twenties and 50 fifties.*

> No: We will need *42 3/4"* lengths of milled steel to complete this job.

> Yes: We will need *forty-two 3/4"* lengths of milled steel...

or

> We will need *42 three-quarter-inch* lengths of milled steel...

☞ **Never begin a sentence with a number, unless it's a year date.** It looks funny to begin a sentence with a number, like starting with a lower-case letter instead of a capital. Spell out the number or rewrite the sentence:

Ninety thousand shares of XYZ flooded the market.

XYZ flooded the market by selling off *90,000 shares.*

☞ **Use figures for all amounts of money.** I strongly recommend this because in business writing, you can't afford to be ambiguous and inexact with dollars—or pesos, or pounds. Numerals are clear and unequivocal, and they make a stronger and more durable visual impression than words. While it may make sense to write "fifty cents" in a novel, a bank customer can far more easily comprehend and remember "a $.50 service charge fee" than "a fifty-cent service charge fee." And look at the difference in clarity (and length) between these two sentences:

Sebastian requested an advance of *five hundred and forty-five thousand, seven hundred and fifty dollars.*

Sebastian requested an advance of *$545,750.*

To write out such a number is obviously dumb and unreasonable.

In general, whole numbers of dollars should be expressed without the decimal point and two zeros:

We will charge *$25* to reconnect your service.
Three days of defensive driving school will cost *$750* per participant.

However, if you are dealing with a series of mixed dollar amounts (dollars and cents), it's customary to express them all in the same form:

> The company sells the RQ 100 model for *$49.95*;
> the RQ 150 sells for *$75.00*.

Other exceptions to this convention are dollar and loan amounts in loan and mortgage agreements, wills, and other legal documents, in which exact amounts are critical:

> Title will be transferred concurrent with payment
> of the sum of *$7,400.00* to Mr. Hugh Dixon.

> You will make 104 payments of *$123.00* each.

☞ **Use a comma between groups of three numbers except in year dates.** I'm sure you do this automatically:

> Her estate is estimated to exceed *$14,000,000*.

> I asked her to invoice us in advance for *2,000*
>   copies of the report.

Occasionally people are tempted to omit the comma in a number in the thousands.

Resist the temptation and reserve the no-comma convention for year dates:

> No: The company now employs over *1000* analysts.

> Yes: The company now employs over *1,000* analysts.

> But: Our computers dealt ably with the year *2000.*

> In *1945,* butter was scarce all over the country.

☞ **In most cases, write days of the month as numerals.** February 23, 1979. That's just the way it's done. Although dates are pronounced as ordinals (the descriptive, *-st, -nd, -rd* forms of numbers), don't write September 23rd or June 1st:

> On *September 23, 2004,* the organization was incorporated.

> May we expect a decision by *June 1?*

However, you may use the ordinal forms if the order of the date is inverted, or if no month is specified:

We are closed on *the fourth of July.*

I will expect your answer before *the 21st.*

☞ **If you wish to write out numbers above nine.** If you do need to write them out as words, the numbers twenty-one through twenty-nine, thirty-one through thirty-nine, and so on, up through ninety-one through ninety-nine, are hyphenated. The rest: one hundred, one thousand, one hundred thousand, are written without hyphens. The ordinals—twenty-first through twenty-ninth, and so on, work the same way

> *Thirty-eight thousand* runners participated in the *one hundredth* running of the Boston Marathon .

☞ **Follow this rule for fractions.** Leave fractions open when they are nouns, hyphenate them as adjectives:

Noun: Fidelity placed *one half* of the Salem
             municipal bonds traded in May.

Adjective: We need a *two-thirds majority* to carry
             the resolution.

☞ **Express the time of day as a number.** Again, this recommendation is specific to business writing: you're less likely to be misunderstood and more likely to be remembered:

I've scheduled the meeting for *7:45 p.m.*

Kate will be here before *9:00* and after *11:30.*

☞ **Don't create hybrid forms in a range of inclusive numbers.** When you want to express the idea of duration or inclusion within a certain range of numbers, you have a couple of options. If, for example, your intern Josh was in a management seminar over five days, you have at least three acceptable ways of expressing the fact:

Josh attended the seminar January *1-5.*

Josh attended the seminar *from* January 1 *to* January *5.*

Josh attended the seminar *between* January 1 *and* January *5.*

The first form, with the hyphen, is informal, the others stricter style. The pitfall inherent in having choices is that people often unwisely try to combine two styles. You should not write, for example:

Josh attended the seminar *from January 1-5*

or

Josh attended the seminar *between January 1-5.*

Either go with the hyphen and no words or use both words: *from...to, between...and.*

On the subject of inclusive numbers—that is, numbers covering a range and separated with an en dash—there are some incredibly complicated rules for when to write all the numbers each time: pages 111–117, for example, you may abbreviate as 111–17 instead of 111–117, but you must write 100–104. I vote for simplifying by writing all the numbers out all the time. If you're interested, *The Chicago Manual of Style* covers the subject exhaustively (see Appendix F for this and other recommended books).

APPENDIX C

A WORD ABOUT YOUR PC

You probably write on a desktop PC or laptop, using one of the standard word processing programs. Most of these include tools you can use to help improve your prose, but you must take them with what my great-aunt Jane, whose life was a monument to malapropisms, used to call "a dose of salts." You must under no circumstances rely on them to eliminate writing errors. I'm not denying they can help, but the computer cannot think the way a person does. Sorry: a computer cannot think at all. (At least not yet.) Here are some recommendations for making use of the strengths while avoiding the weaknesses of these tools.

☞ **Grammar checkers.** Grammar checkers flag such common errors as disagreement, sentence fragments, and overreliance on passive construction. Given the complexity of our language, it's amazing that they work at all, and I don't think they work very well. The Grammar tool on my toolbar can't distinguish between the two uses of *many* in the following sentences, for example:

> *Many* thanks for agreeing to represent Foss
> Brothers.

> Some of these parts are built to spec, but *many* are
> not.

Grammar suggested that the former sentence should read "Many *thank...*" I don't think so. Do you see what I mean?

Naturally, because programming is an all-or-nothing business, Grammar is hypervigilant. This can be deeply annoying. The moment it runs across any form of the verb *to be*, it starts objecting to passive construction. For example, Grammar chides me for writing

> I'm concerned by my poor credit record,

suggesting instead

> My poor credit record concerns me.

That puts the emphasis on the credit record, which isn't what I wanted. Though I've urged you not to overuse the passive voice, you're better off running your own check than having Grammar wag a finger every time you say, "I am pleased," or "I'm concerned."

Sometimes a call is just plain wrong, often almost inexplicably. My favorite investment advisor, noting that the stock market could go as high as it's ever gone, wrote in his newsletter, "That in itself is a dramatic thought." Grammar changed "itself" to "it."

And pity the young man whose grammar checker convinced him to write contributors, including me, to his recent fundraising effort, "I *rose* over $5,000." The checker didn't care for "raise." Why ask why?

Bottom line: grammar checkers can be helpful, but they have clear limitations. Stay tuned. Somewhere out there, perhaps in a humble garage, Weird Stanley, the Programmer Who Has No Life, is developing a version that can deal with all these shortcomings and more.

☞ **Spell checkers.** You've probably experienced the limitations of these tools already. Spell checkers can set you right if you misspell a word: they're all over *acommodate, accomodate,* and *acommoddate.* They'll set you straight, and they've been creatively programmed to figure out what you were trying to spell. But they don't have a hope if you misuse a word. Homonyms—words that sound alike but have different meanings and spellings—are all the same to them. *Their, there,* and *they're* are equally acceptable to my spell checker. And it's perfectly content with such atrocities as

> Legal council argues that this elicit behavior
> mitigates against hiring are allusive applicant.

It's also unable to recognize the nonsense created by extraneous words, often the result of hasty editing:

> I must get a flight to for Detroit immediately for
> Detroit.

(Interestingly, Grammar finds nothing wrong with that sentence, either, and gives it excellent scores for readability.) I also suspect the fine hand of a spell checker in Sebastian Junger's book, *The Perfect Storm*. The South Shore of Massachusetts boasts a nice town called Scituate. In early editions of the book, the name of the town was changed to Situate. I rest my case.

On the plus side, my spell checker lifts my spirits with some astonishing suggestions for proper names it doesn't recognize, offering "carboy" for "Kirby" and archly recommending "hoyden" for "Hayden." This is almost more fun than solitaire. And equally useful.

☞ **Grade or reading level indicators.** Your software may include various types of readability gauges, alone or as part of your grammar checker. The five or six I've seen scan your piece for variables such as word length and passive constructions. By collating the data, they arrive at a numerical score that supposedly reflects the readability of your prose.

The late Robert Gunning's Fog Index is as reliable as any, but it's helpful only if you can interpret the results: my program simply gives me a score with no explanation. I offered it two paragraphs, one very simple, one very difficult, and received respective scores of 0 and 30. This paragraph scored a 13.2; random paragraphs in this book tend to land between 8 and 12. If your Gunning Fog Index came without an explanation, this gives you an idea of where to aim.

Readability indexes aren't entirely dependable. I understand one of them gave Lincoln's Gettysburg Address and a passage from Mark Twain's *Huckleberry Finn* very bad reviews. As if. The message: use readability indexes if you like, but don't let them push you around.

☞ **Find and Replace Commands.** Most word processing software helps you quickly find and replace a word you've used, presumably because you're having second thoughts about it. Remember if you use your Replace tool that it will replace a word but may leave extraneous material behind, such as a final *s*, if you've made a possessive plural, that is no longer appropriate. Another problem is that most Replace commands will not replace any word that has a punctuation mark after it, no matter how you instruct them, because they don't recognize the word with the punctuation as the same word you're asking to replace. So if you're replacing, you're going to have to run a spell check, and you probably should read through the text yourself as well. In other words, you might as well have used the Find command and replaced the words yourself one by one. As for Find, if you accidentally insert a space in the Find What box (it's hard to see when you've done it), your program will not be able to find the word or phrase unless the word in text happens to have an extra space in the same place.

☞ **Thesauruses.** (Yes, it's correct; "thesauri" is also correct.) You may remember that I encourage you elsewhere in the book to go ahead and use your word of first choice, rather than trying to find new words for the same thing. I have not changed my mind. Reading work that's clearly been subjected to the Thesaurus command only confirms my opinion.

Some wag has asserted that there are only two exact synonyms in the English language— "furze" and "gorse." That's a little hard to believe, but it makes a point: there are almost always subtle shades of meaning between similar words. Replacing your word by a so-called synonym suggested by Thesaurus is not as easy as it may seem. For one thing, a verb or preposition used with one of the words may not be correct with the other. Example: My thesaurus gives "notice" as a synonym for "attention." However, the two words differ in usage. We say, "I *paid* no attention *to* him"; but we say, "I *took* no notice *of* him." If you change "attention" to "notice," you've written "I paid no notice to him." If you think that sounds good, buying this book was a waste of money. I'm sorry to report that I've come upon such blunders many times. It's usually pretty obvious that the writer has been calling up wannabe synonyms by this method.

Peter Mark Roget, the eponymous author of *Roget's Thesaurus*, did not, interestingly enough, set out to write a book of synonyms. He was born in 1779, in a century that was obsessed with classification, from Carolus Linnaeus's comprehensive cataloguing of plants and animals to Samuel Johnson's monumental *Dictionary of the English Language*, and it was his bright idea that words could be classified in families in the same way. He never viewed his book as a synonym finder. Remember this when you're tempted to abuse your thesaurus. Incidentally, mine just choked, as it were, suggesting that perhaps I meant "gorge yourself."for "gorse." Sigh.

I have a point, which is that all these tools, though they can be useful, can also waste your time. Worse, if you are foolish enough to depend upon them, they can give you a false sense of security. As of this writing, they're no substitute for your own thoughtful editing.

A SPECIAL SITUATION: RESPONDING TO CUSTOMER COMPLAINT LETTERS

Since no organization is perfect, inevitably you'll get them—the dreaded letters of complaint. Here are some tips to ensure that your response satisfies the writer of a complaint to you or to your organization.

☞ **Follow a policy of responding immediately to a complaint.** Remember, your writer is already dissatisfied and has gone to some trouble to write and send a message. The only payback in delaying your answer is increased resentment. If you're charged with responding to a complaint, don't wait. If you can't get into the issue immediately, or if the problem is particularly complex , write or phone the customer to say you've received the letter and will be responding as soon as possible.

Sometimes in large organizations, a letter of complaint immediately prompts a form letter signed by a member of senior management, often the president. This letter goes out immediately to the customer via e-mail or the post office, expressing thanks for his or her communication and voicing assurances that the matter is being looked into. It doesn't need to be long (see First Response to Customer Complaint, page 203). The form letter is followed up quickly by a letter that specifically addresses the issue(s) the customer has raised.

☞ Read the customer's letter very, very carefully.

You want to be sure you understand just what has upset the person and interpret what the letter says as accurately as possible. Try to keep your own feelings and projections out of your reading so you don't overreact or respond to an issue that hasn't even been raised. Be sure you completely understand the problem or problems: often a letter highlights more than one.

☞ Remind yourself that your customer is your superior.

Business texts make the point that your customer is by definition up the organizational chain from you. Use the information in Chapter 3 to generate a tone that is respectful and polite. Never blame or belittle a customer—even a customer who is wrong. That's just not good politics.

☞ Look at the issue from the customer's viewpoint. It's

no use telling the customer that slow service reflects recent layoffs designed to save the company money. That's writer-centered, and it's just going to anger the customer further. Avoid references to job productivity, performance goals, and other similar concepts that reflect the organization's viewpoint. Concentrate, instead, on the effect on the customer: his or her feelings, convenience, time wasted, money lost, etc. In this way, you can project empathy that goes a long way toward defusing anger.

☞ **Try to understand where the letter is coming from.** Here's where a little armchair psychology can help you. Learn all you can about the writer through his or her letter. By reading thoughtfully, you can get inside the writer's head, and this may tell you whether the person is

> rational
> lonely
> hostile and taking it out on you
> well educated
> crazy (it happens: be careful)
> young and inexperienced
> old and puzzled

and tailor your response accordingly.

☞ **Be aware that you are documenting, on behalf of yourself and your organization.** Don't write anything you may later regret. Remember that your reply represents a commitment. If you agree to a condition the customer requests, or offer a rebate or reimbursement by way of apology, be sure your organization will stand behind you.

☞ **Explain why you are the person responding if the customer's letter was written to someone else.** Most letters are written to senior management; most are answered by someone less senior. Show why you are the appropriate person to answer the letter:

> Because I'm in charge of environmental
> compliance at BCX, Mr. Henshaw has forwarded
> your letter to me, and I am pleased to have the
> chance to respond to your concerns.

☞ **Show you understand by walking the customer through the episode(s).** Let's say, for example, you handle complaints for a brokerage firm. A customer placed a stock trade that somehow was not completed, called to inquire about it and was first put on hold, then disconnected. Reflect each part of the experience back to the customer in your letter:

> I understand that you placed a trade for 2,000
> shares of NetWorth on December 18 at 10:00 a.m.
> Apparently, our organization failed to complete
> your trade. The next day, NetWorth rose 46
> points, or 50 percent. When you called on
> December 21 to sell, you discovered the trade had
> never been placed. And when you asked to speak
> to a supervisor, your call was delayed and
> ultimately disconnected…

People sometimes object when I tell them to do this. They are afraid the customer will only get increasingly riled up if they start going over the ground again. I disagree, because I've spoken with a number of customers about this technique, and virtually all endorse it. It confirms that someone has read their letter with care. It also serves as an acknowledgment of what took place, which will lead to an explanation, at least, if not an apology. For the example above, let's hope someone can produce one eloquent enough to forestall a lawsuit.

☞ **Explain what happened and why.** Your reader will appreciate a well-reasoned explanation of the episode. You should take particular care to pitch this explanation to a level that's understandable to someone outside the organization. No jargon, no telescoping of procedures: remember the Dangerous Level of Knowledge. Your reader doesn't know this material the way you do.

☞ **Be open rather than defensive. If your organization blew it, apologize.** This advice, which I've given before, is worth repeating. Nobody's perfect, and you and your company are no exception. It's painful to have to admit to a mistake. But from the customer's standpoint, it's much easier to forgive someone who is openly and sincerely apologizing than someone making excuses. Trying to cover up or justify an error only makes the problem worse and the customer angrier.

Be sure, if your customer has two gripes, that you apologize for both.

☞ **Try to give the customer something if you've caused a problem.** Of course you'd substitute a product that works for one that doesn't. If you overcharged, you'll refund or rebate the charge. And if there may still be any possible confusion or questions in the customer's mind, you'll give your phone number or that of someone down the chain so the customer will have an immediate contact within the organization.

But consider, in addition, especially if you've caused real inconvenience, the possibility of giving the customer something—in short, a present. Some organizations have small gifts ready to give out in such situations, from digital clocks to mouse pads to t-shirts printed with the company logo. It's not so much the value of the item as the symbolic gesture of good will. Other companies will reduce a price or payment if the customer has been seriously inconvenienced. A dreadful clerk in a department store once gave me a general runaround that included rude behavior and inaccurate information about the item I wanted to buy. I finally took the item to the manager, who apologized wholeheartedly, then rang up the item for me at half price. He hoped he said it would in some measure make up for the inconvenience I had suffered. And it did. About 100 percent. Money makes a lot of problems go away: consider it when you want to assuage a complaint.

☞ **Take steps within your organization so this won't happen again.** Well, so it's at least less likely to happen again. Your job's not over when you've resolved the problem to a customer's satisfaction. A customer's complaint may also signal a weakness within some area of your business or company that if addressed could improve your performance overall. If appropriate, you may want to forward the complaint to whoever's responsible for the management of that area. A customer writing about a poorly performing product, for example, could help alert a company to problems on its production line. If a customer complains about incompetent service, the complaint could point to larger issues of hiring practices, adequate staffing, or proper training.

First Response to Customer Complaint
(form letter with blanks filled in)

Xavier Marine Products
412 Lynn Avenue
Seattle, Washington 98199

March 17, 20__

Mr. Jacob Goodwin
3906 Indian Lane
Washington, DC 20008

Dear Mr. Goodwin:

Thank you for your letter of March 16, in which you express concerns about our global positioning system, which apparently directed you into a cranberry bog instead of the Cape Cod canal. Because at Xavier Marine Products we are eager to deliver the best possible service to our customers, we appreciate it when a customer who experiences problems calls them to our attention. We are looking into the matter, and you can expect to hear from us within a week.

Sincerely,

Bert Samuelson, President
Xavier Marine Products

Response to Customer Complaint

Third Citizens Bank
800 Washington Boulevard
Minneapolis, Minnesota

August 22, 20—

Ms. Lucy Robbins
252 Overlook Drive
Hyde Park, NY 12538

Dear Ms. Robbins:

Thank you for your recent letter to Third Citizens. I am sorry that you have been perplexed regarding the figure owed and the late payment charge on your instalment loan account. And I apologize sincerely, on behalf of Citizens, for the difficult time you have had trying to get a satisfactory explanation to the problem. The enclosed account payment history should help answer some of your questions.

You asked why you owe $102.73 and why you are being charged for a late payment. On this type of loan, additional funds received are not applied to the balance but are credited toward the next scheduled payment. On June 4, 20__, we received your check (number 1435) for $521.73. The amount due was $309.73, leaving extra funds of $212.00. This extra amount was "rolled over" toward your next payment date, leaving $97.73

due to complete a full payment. A late charge of $5.00 was added to that $97.73, bringing the total amount due to complete that partial payment to $102.73. This is why you are receiving letters requesting that amount.

I apologize for the inconvenience you experienced when you telephoned on July 15, were put on hold, waited for 20 minutes, and ultimately received no satisfactory answer to your questions. I have spoken with the customer service representatives on duty that day, reminding them of their obligation to be helpful and courteous to all customers. We also reviewed the procedure for instalment loan overpayments and late charges, to help ensure that others are served properly in the future. Thank you for bringing the matter to our attention. Although we try to give our customers excellent service, despite our best efforts, we occasionally fall short of our goal, as we evidently did on this occasion. Again, my apologies.

If you have further questions about your loan payments, please call me at any time. My telephone number is 602-374-3206.

Sincerely,

Katherine Smallzell
Vice President

MEMO AND LETTER TIPS AND FORMATS

Whether sent electronically, by fax, or by mail, memos and letters represent your organization. It's therefore enormously important that they be of good quality.

If your organization has formats you're asked to follow, so much the better. If not, and particularly if people are doing their own thing and stuff is being sent around to other departments or into the outside world at the whim of individual writers, you may want to standardize letter and memo formats. This saves time, once everyone knows exactly what's expected. No one needs to dig out the Gregg manual that was right there on the receptionist's desk before she went on vacation. You'll present an image of yourselves as well organized and in control. (Your Internet service provider has its own way of dealing with the elements of a memo—To and From, attachments, etc. Just play along.)

The following tips will remind you of what readers deserve in a memo or letter, whether it's e-mailed or sent overland. And the sample formats reflect my thinking about what looks nice, observing what various organizations do, and selectively checking out secretarial handbooks and business style manuals. Most of these give any number of possible formats: there really isn't one "correct" form. Choose one and stick with it. I happen to like these two.

Tips for Memo Writing

- Make certain your subject heading is explanatory—a headline, not a title.

- Keep to a single subject whenever possible.

- Try to limit your memo to a single page of type.

- Put points in logical sequence. Be accurate and specific with details.

- Since a memo is typically an internal communication, your language should pass the read-aloud test without embarrassing you: make it simple and conversational.

- In closing, prompt any necessary action from your reader(s).

- Note any attachment; note copies sent to anyone else.

- Double-check for mechanical errors.

Sample Memo Format

(Letterhead, if desired)
Third Citizens Five Cents Bank, N.A.

(Skip three spaces)
TO:Jane Upshaw
(Skip one space)
FROM:David Thorne
(Skip one space)
SUBJECT:AHSB "Scholarships" Budget
(Skip one space)
DATE:March 2, 20___

(Skip three spaces. Begin body copy, block style, no indent)
I recommend that we earmark approximately $50,000 of next year's Education Required Budget to begin a systematic process of sponsoring two key Citizens staff members as students in the Alexander Hamilton School of Banking (AHSB). As this is a three-year program, we'll need to have a comparable amount allocated in subsequent years (see proposed budget outline, attached).
(Skip one space)
AHSB offers a curriculum designed to provide depth in management ranks. It focuses on bankers with expertise in their own specialized areas and broadens their experiences to include other areas of banking. In addition, the AHSB program requires a thesis, and many participants have apparently used this opportunity to develop frameworks for new programs eventually implemented in their own banks.
(Skip one space)
If you like the idea, I recommend that we ask Mary Dale, John

McAllister, and Arthur Beal to consider areas of their departments where management depth is a concern. Then, either
through an application process or personal recommendations,
we can create a pool of candidates. Final selections can be made
by a panel of Human Resources senior management, in-house
APSB graduates, and line management.
(Skip one space)
Please let me know your thoughts. The deadline for early
admissions is November 15.

(Skip five spaces)

Attachment
(Skip one space)
cc: Eleanor Wu
Dan Paulsen

Tips on Writing Letters

- Use a colon after your salutation, even after a first name.

- Don't waste your opening line: begin graciously.

- Share good news immediately.

- Hold bad news until you've built your case.

- Use "I" and "you" freely, focusing on "you."

- Don't use formal language or outdated business idioms.

- Close politely: suggest next step or contact, then, if appropriate, voice appreciation of reader and indicate your pleasure to serve, help, share.

- Reread your letter for errors, sound effects.

- Reread again to be sure it *clearly* answers the question, "Why this letter?"

Sample Letter Format

(**Letterhead**) CUSTOM STRUCTURED SYSTEMS
3 PINECLIFFE DRIVE, WINCHESTER, ILLINOIS 60914

(**skip 6 spaces**)

June 18, 20__

(**Skip three spaces**)

Mr. Thomas Wright, President
Wright Investments, Inc.
1444 5th Street
Chicago, IL 60912
(**Skip one space**)
Dear Mr. Wright:
(**Skip one space. Begin body copy, block style, no indents**)
I'm delighted to respond to your invitation to undertake work
for Wright Investments. Custom Structured Systems (CSS)
proposes to perform a data processing study and prepare a
report that will recommend the most effective computer system
for Wright. I've enclosed a Statement of Work that describes
the specific tasks CSS will perform as part of this effort.
(**Skip one space**)
Our study will focus on understanding and defining your present and future data processing needs and choosing the computers and applications that best meet those needs.
(**Skip one space**)
We'll analyze Wright's business operations and current systems and evaluate appropriate computers and application programs. Based on our findings, we'll then recommend the most

effective system for Wright and present a detailed plan for an orderly conversion of your existing computer applications.
(Skip one space)
Please let me know whether this proposal meets with your approval. CSS is eager to begin the study, and we look forward to working with Wright.

(Skip two spaces)

Sincerely,

(Skip four spaces)

Martha N. Briedis
Senior Vice President

(Skip two spaces)

MNB/db **(Writer's and secretary's initials, if appropriate)**
(Skip one space)
Enclosure
(Skip one space)
cc **(or *xc* for Xerox copy, or simply *c*)**: George Milholland
Tessa McDermott

APPENDIX F

OTHER BOOKS ON WRITING

Take your pick on amazon.com: there are literally hundreds of books on business writing and on writing in general. Here are a few that I especially like.

Books Targeted Specifically to Business Writing

Alred, Gerald J., Walter E. Oliu, and Charles T. Brusaw. *The Business Writer's Handbook*, 8th ed. New York: St. Martin's Press, 2006. This one's been around for a long time, and reflects good common sense and straightforward advice. It's very thorough, and also kind of a workout, which fits some people's needs: its 650-plus pages include a lot of exercises and examples.

Dumaine, Deborah. *Write to the Top: Writing for Corporate Success*. New York: Random House, Inc., 2004. Short, to the point, upbeat, and easy to read, this book offers practical advice on writing in the business place and amusing examples of bad letters and memos. Among its exercises is a useful set that helps you assess your own writing strengths and weaknesses.

Fielden, John, and Ronald Dulek. *Bottom-Line Business Writing*. Englewood Cliffs, N. J.: Prentice-Hall, Inc., 1983. A short, well-written book with some interesting ideas and theories about what to write to whom and when. Emphatically oriented toward the structure rather than the mechanics of writing, it examines in depth the form and language appropriate for memos, letters, and reports, depending on the relative positions of writer and reader in the organizational hierarchy. It may be out of print, but it's available online.

Geffner, Andrea B. *Business English: a Complete Guide to Developing an Effective Business Style,* 3rd ed. Hauppauge, N.Y.: Barron's Educational Series, 1998. A large, informative paperback, written for a general business audience, this book spends a lot of time on the elementary: parts of speech, principles of grammar and punctuation, how to spell the plurals of words ending in *s*, and the like. Lots of exercises, with answers, reinforce its guidelines. It also includes dozens of model letters, memos, and reports on very specific topics: Letter Declining a Job Offer, Credit-Refusing Letter, even a business Letter of Condolence.

Books on Writing in General

Associated Press. *The Associated Press Stylebook and Libel Manual,* revised and updated. New York: Basic Books (Perseus), 2004. I don't recommend this as an all-round bible. It works well if you're a journalist, no doubt, but the style is less strict than most manuals recommend for business use. Relaxed style may work well for a newspaper or magazine, but it could get you into trouble on the job. Compare your morning paper and you'll see what I mean: most major dailies make inconsistent use of the serial comma, drops the *s* after possessive nouns ending in *s*, and in general commits errors you don't want to make.

On the other hand, the AP Stylebook section gives a tremendous amount of useful information on treatment of words and names, pointing out that Hovercraft is a trademark, that the U.S. Census divides the Northeast region into the New England and the Middle Atlantic states, and that *prior to* is a stilted version of *before*. In addition to the Libel Manual, it includes, among other things, a short but helpful glossary of business terms.

Bernstein, Theodore M. *The Careful Writer*. New York: Free Press, l993. This book is wonderful and informative, a pleasure to read for its own sake. The late Theodore Bernstein, a widely respected author and editor,was a star in the pantheon of writing experts, and his writing is funny as well as authoritative. His commonsense approach seems as reasonable as it did when the book first appeared in 1965. *The Careful Writer* is encyclopedic in form—that is, it goes from A to Z—and I virtually always find what I'm looking for in it. Did you know the word *deficient* takes the preposition *in*? or that *postpone* and *delay* don't mean the same thing? Read this and learn more.

Buckley, William. *The Right Word*. Selected, assembled, and edited by Samuel S. Vaughan. New York: Random House, 1996. The feisty former editor of *National Review* as revealed, in correspondence, interviews, fiction, and essays, with his take on words from every angle: punctuation, usage, gender-blind writing, dictionaries, and faxing and e-mailing—you name it. Approximately one hundred pages comprise a "Buckley Lexicon": anyone who'd like to build a more graceful vocabulary should take note. Buckley yields to no one in the elegance with which he expresses himself.

Chicago Manual of Style, 15th ed. Chicago: University of Chicago Press, 2003. Probably the ultimate in authoritative, classic guides to direct the user in writing a book or thesis—from its inception, through the complexities of tables of contents, footnotes, and indexes, to publication. For us all, it offers the last word on capitalization, forms of address for members of governments around the world, punctuation (20 different sections on use of the comma and 13 pages on the hyphen). It's very well indexed and thorough; for business purposes, it probably offers more than you need to know, but it's an invaluable resource.

Fowler, H.W. *A Dictionary of Modern English Usage.* 3rd ed., edited by R.W. Burchfield. Oxford: Oxford University Press, l996. Another classic, this one revised and updated. The first edition, published in 1926 and revised by Ernest Gowers (1965) reflected the author's unique take on usage and method of indexing, which included such entries as "Airs and graces" and "Pleonastic humor." This mode of organization has always made it hard to find what you're looking for in Fowler. The new edition has simplified getting around the book somewhat, but it has been faulted for laxity in style: its acceptance of "impact" as a verb, for example, and "hopefully" meaning "it is to be hoped." Many of the original, quirky Fowlerisms remain, and the book is fun for browsing.

Harbrace College Handbook, edited by, John C. Hodges. l2th ed. New York: Harcourt, l995. A serviceable and comprehensive text focusing on grammar, style, and usage. Many other large publishing houses issue similar ones, also well done. There's more basic information in them than you may need, but it's all there if you do.

Johnson, Edward. *The Handbook of Good English.* New York: Washington Square Press, 1991. I stumbled accidentally on this thorough and carefully written handbook on grammar, style, and usage and now use it quite often. Edward Johnson's systems of sections confuses me a little, but that may be my fault for always being in a hurry. His inclusive glossary, which also functions as an index, helps. The book contains a lot of excellent information covered in painstaking detail.

Safire, William. *How Not to Write: The Essential Misrules of Grammar,* New York: W. W. Norton, 2005. Any of Safire's books is a treat. The *New York Times* columnist is arguably the most widely read writer on language in the world. His Sunday columns don't hesitate to take on the thorniest issues of English usage. If you want to read about jargon, slang, dialect, or new words, you'll find Safire's books witty and enjoyable. In *On Language,* 1980, and *No Uncertain Terms,* 2003, he blends material from his columns with letters from readers to entertaining effect.

Strunk, William and E.B White, with a foreword by Roger Angell. *The Elements of Style,* 4th ed. New York: Longman Publishers, 2000. Some things don't change, among them Strunk and White. It's timeless. Strunk and White, as it's known, hits the high spots of writing in general in just 92 pages of clear, sensible prose. The book is particularly targeted to college students, for whom it was originally written, but the advice applies to all types of writing.

Tarshis, Barry. *Grammar for Smart People.* New York: Pocketbooks, 1993. A newsletter editor I do business with swears by this one for grammar and punctuation. Barry Tarshis writes appealingly and straightforwardly. An easy read, well targeted for a business audience.

Turabian, Kate. *A Manual for Writers of Term Papers, Theses, and Dissertations,* 6th ed. Chicago: University of Chicago Press, 1996. A short paperback based on the *Chicago Manual of Style,* this book contains easy-to-understand, decisive information. Spelling and Punctuation, and Capitalization, Underlining, and Other Matters of Style are among its most useful chapters. The punctuation sections are particularly complete and comprehensible. Offered as "the definitive guide on correct style for formal papers," the book is obviously meant for scholars, and one can't follow its guidelines to the letter in all types of business writing (advertising, for example), but it provides an excellent base from which to start.

Words Into Type, 4th ed., edited by Thomas L. Warren. Englewood Cliffs: Prentice-Hall, Inc., 1992. Get this one for the office. My third edition (based on studies by Marjorie Skillen *et al.*) has served me so well I'm going to stick with it. A fairly expensive hardcover book, it bails me out when I run into tough editing problems, be they ever so tiny or downright weird. Where else can you find nearly a page cataloguing nouns with two different plurals, or the proper abbreviations for all the Canadian provinces? My *Words Into Type* includes a large section on grammar; long and helpful lists on such subjects as Trite Expressions, Words and Phrases Often Used Superfluously, Foreign Words and Phrases; and a 14-page section on The Right Preposition! To add to its charms, the book is indexed in a way that seems both complete and intuitive.

Zinsser, William. *On Writing Well: An Informal Guide to Writing Nonfiction*, 5th ed. New York: Harper/Collins Publishers, 2001. Open any page and you'll be hooked. Everyone seems to love Mr. Zinsser's prose: this book has been on everyone's recommended list for decades. His examples of writing are lively as well as instructive, and he has a chapter on business writing that glows with wisdom.

Dictionaries

American Heritage Dictionary of the English Language, 4th ed. Boston: Houghton Mifflin Company, 2000. This inclusive 90,000-word dictionary (that's big) features the recommendations of the Usage Panel, including the percentages who advocate or shun a particular element of style or usage. The Usage Panel comprises a collection of writers, editors, and other experts, and its notes, uniformly lively and interesting, represent an admirable blend of tradition and common sense.

Merriam-Webster's Collegiate Dictionary, 11th ed. Springfield, MA: Merriam-Webster, 2003. This is the short version of *Webster's Third New International Unabridged Dictionary* and is the choice of the *Chicago Manual of Style* for all questions of spelling and word division. That's good enough for me. It has the additional charm of telling you when a word came into use: the word *business* has been with us since the 14th century, *technology*, believe it or not, since 1859 (when it no doubt meant the McCormick Reaper). *Webster's Collegiate* also gives long and very helpful lists of words with prefixes such as *pre-* and *non-* that it suggests not hyphenating. Make everyone in the department use this dictionary: you'll present a consistent image because you'll all be, literally, on the same page.

INDEX

a
  with abbreviations,
    acronyms, 196–198
  with number, 136
  as well as, 133–134
abbreviations
  with *a* or *an*, 197
  identifying, 196–197
  periods (points) with, 162,
    164, 197–198
  plurals of, 161–162
abstract words, use of,
  173–178
acronyms, 162–163, 197–198
action, keeping in verbs, 74–75
active versus passive verbs,
  45–51
addresses, written with
  numerals, 213
adverbs, 158, 193–196
adverse, averse, 53
affect, effect, 53
affect, impact, 64–65
age, discriminatory references
  to, 126
agreement
  of pronoun with subject,

97–107
  of verb with subject,
    128–132, 138–140
alliteration, accidental, 87
almost, 196
alot, 67
alright, 67
although, 20
ambiguous, ambivalent, 57
among, between, 58
amount, number, 57
ampersand (&), 198–199
an with abbreviations,
  acronyms, 197
anybody, anyone, 138
any time, anytime, 53
apology, 10, 32–33, 231
apostrophe, 98–99,159–162
as if, 61
as, like, 61
as well as, 133–134
averse, adverse, 53

bad news, organizing to
  write, 3–5, 12, 18–20
be, to, 46, 51, 18–20
better, 183

between, among, 58
between ... and, 219–220
Big Top method of organiza-
    tion, 12–18
bit, a, 26
Black Hole School of
    Writing, 73
brackets, 171
brevity, editing for, 68–75
bring, take, 58
bullets, 22
business idioms, outdated, 32
but, 20, 94–95

capital, Capitol, capitol, 53
capital letters
    with abbreviations,
        196–197
    use of, 190–193
case, pronoun, 97–107
chronological method of
    organization, 16–17
Chronologically Challenged
    Tiny Person School of
    Writing, 110
clichés, 82–85
collective nouns, 135–137
colon, 153–154
comma
    inside quotation marks,
        164–165
    in numbers, 216–217

in sentences, 146–153,
    186–187
compare to, compare with,
    53–54
comparisons
    illogical, 182–183
    unfinished, 183–184
complaint letters, responding
    to, 10, 227–235
complement, compliment, 54, 57
comprise, compose, 58–59
concrete words, use of,
    173–178
conditional verb forms, 25
conjunctions
    beginning sentences with,
        94–95
    linking independent clauses,
        20–21
"connective tissue," 20–21
contact, 173, 174–175
continual, continuous, 54
could, 25
council, counsel, 54

"Dangerous Level of
    Knowledge" (DLK), 6–8,
    20–21
dangling participles and
    modifiers, 186–188
dash, 154–155
dates, numerals with, 213,

216–218
deadline, 211
deductive organization, 12–17
deem, 32
descriptive clause,
    63–64
discriminatory writing, avoid-
    ing, 120–127
do, 45, 74
dollar symbol ($), 199
"don't use 'ems," 199–200
double negative, 70–71

each, 138
educational level of reader, 5
effect, affect, 53
either, neither, 138
e.g., 60
elders, 126
e-mail, 14, 37, 39–44
em dash, 154
emoticons, 41
employee, 123
en dash, 155
enormity, 59
ensure, insure, 54–55
enthuse, 66
equipment, 173
ethnic labels, offensive,
    125–126
even, 195
event, 175–176

every, 138
everybody, everyone, 138
evoke, invoke, 59
exclamation point, 172

facility, 173, 174
fact is that, the, 69–70
false series, 113–119
farther, further, 55, 183
fewer, less, 60
figuratively, literally, 61–62
field of, the, 69
Find command, 225
first, second, third, 21
flounder, founder, 55
formal business language, 32
fractions, writing out, 214,
    218
from … to, 219–220
fulsome, 60
function, 173
further, farther, 55, 183

gender-blind writing
    of names, 124
    of occupations and posi-
        tions, 122–123
    of titles and pronouns,
        121–122
    vocabulary for, 123–124
generalizations, avoiding, 30
good news, organizing to

write, 2–3, 12–18
grammar checker, 221–223
Gunning Fox Index, 224–225

heading, memo, 14
Heaving Bosom School of
  Writing, 191
heighth, 67
homonyms and spell check-
  ers, 223
however, 20, 96
humor, role of in business
  writing, 36–38
hyphen, 156–159
  in numbers, 218

I-focused writing, 9–11
i.e., 60
impact, 64, 173
imply, infer, 60
in addition to, 134
incent, 67
incentivize, 65
individual, 60
inductive organization, 3–5,
  12, 18–20
infer, imply, 60
infinitive, split, 91–92
-ing verb form (participle), 25
in regards to, 67
insure, ensure, 54–55
invoke, evoke, 59

irregardless, 67
it is, 69
its, it's, 98

jargon, 7, 57
just, 194–195

kids, 126
kindly, 31
knowledge, reader's level of,
  5–8

language
  avoiding outdated, 32
  concrete versus abstract,
    173–178
  tone of, 29–32
lay, lie, 61
less, fewer, 60
letters
  of complaint, responding
    to, 10, 32–33, 227–235
  sample, 233–235
  tips on writing, 240
level, hitting the reader's, 5–8
lie, lay, 61
like, as, 61
literally, figuratively, 61–62

majority, 136
malapropisms, 52–67
manipulation of reader, 27–29

may, might, 62
memo
  heading for, 14
  sample, 238–239
  tips on writing, 237
metaphors, mixed, 185
might, may, 62
modifiers
  avoiding between subject
    and verb, 129, 131
  dangling, 186–188
  used with strong adjec-
    tives, 26–27
money
  numerals with, 215–216
  symbols for ($), 199
moreover, 150–151
myself, 101–102

name(s)
  Capitalization of proper,
    190–191
  and gender-blind writing,
    124–125
  using readers', 28–29
negative, double, 70–71
negative tone, 24
negative words, 24
neither, either, 138
neutral news, organizing to
  write, 12–18
nobody, no one, 138

"noise," avoiding unintentional, 86–89
noisome, 62
none, 138–139
nonrestrictive clause, 63–64
nor, 134–135
nother, 67
nouns
  apostrophe with,
    159,161–162
  collective, 135–139
  keeping references to
    clear, 181–182
  turning verbs into, 74–75
"no-way" statements,
  188–189
number, a or *the* with, 137
number, amount, 57
numbers
  inclusive, 219–220
  plurals of, 161–162
  symbol for (#), 199
  to clarify points in writing,
    22
numerals, when to use,
  212–220

occupations, gender-blind
  language for, 122–123
one of those things, 139–140
only, 193–194
or, 134–135

order of words, phrases,
    21–22
ordinals, 217
organizational methods
    for bad news, 3–5, 12,
        18–20
    for good or neutral news,
        2–3, 12–18
    from easy to difficult,
        21–22
    with bullets and number-
        ing, 22
    with connectors, 20
    with order, 21
    otherwise, 150
outdated language, 32

paragraphs
    organization of, 14–18
    varying length of, 76–78
parallel construction,
    113–119
parentheses, 170–171
participle
    dangling, 186–188
    present, 25
passive versus active verbs,
    45–51
patronizing language, 29–31
pedal, peddle, 55–56
percentage, 136
period, 162–163, 164

physical impairments, refer-
    ences to, 126–127
plurals
    and subject-verb agree-
        ment, 133–141
    of abbreviations and num-
        bers, 161–162
point of view, 23–24
possessives
    apostrophe with, 159–161
    of pronouns, 98–99
prepositions
    ending sentences with,
        92–94
    pileup of, 71–73
principal, principle, 56
pronouns
    agreement of, 98, 99
    correct case of, 99–100
    correct number of,
        100–101
    frequently misused,
        101–106
    gender-blind, 121–122
    keeping references to
        clear, 180–181
    possessive form of, 98
punctuation marks
    apostrophe, 98–99,
        159–162
    brackets, 171–172
    colon, 153–154

comma, 146–153
dash, em and en 154–155
exclamation point, 172
hyphen, 156–159
parentheses, 170–171
period, 162–163
quotation marks, 163–166
semicolon, 150, 166–168
slash or virgule, 168–169
pyramid, inverted pyramid
  methods of organization,
  12–20

qualifiers, limiting, 26–27
quotation marks, double and
  single, 163–166

racial labels, offensive,
  125–126
re: in memo, 14–15
rather, 26
readability indexes, 224–225
reader-centered writing, 1–2
  and *I* messages, 11
  and level of knowledge,
  5–8
  of good and bad news, 2–5
redundancies
  avoiding, 110–111
  list of commonly used, 111
reflexive pronouns, 101–102
relationship, 173, 175

relatively, 27
repetition of words, 108–112
Replace command, 225
restrictive clauses, 63–64
rhyme, unintentional, 88–89
Rock Bottom method of
  organization, 12, 18–20

saving, savings, 56
select, selected, 62
semicolon, 150, 166–168
seniors, 126
sentence(s)
  beginning with conjunc-
  tion, 94–95
  beginning with number,
  214–215
  ending with preposition,
  92–94
  form of, 78–79
  length of, 78
  structure of, 113–119,
  128–132
sexist writing, avoiding,
  121–125
shall, will, 63
should, 25
sic, 171
situation, 173
slash, 168–169
somebody, someone, 138
somewhat, 26

"sound effects," unintentional, 86–89
spell checker, 223–224
split infinitive, 91–92
subject(s)
   keeping near verb, 128–132
   number, agreement of, 100–101, 129–131
subjunctive mood, 142, 145
such as, 61
symbols: &, #, $, %, 198–199
synonyms, 109–110, 225–226

take, bring, 58
teens, 126
template as writing aid, 207–208
tentative writing, 25–27
that, which, 63–64
there are, there is, 69
therefore, 22, 150
thesaurus command, 225–226
to be, 46, 51, 74–75
to do, 45, 74–75
tone of writing, 23–38
   apology and, 32–33
   humor and, 36–38
   manipulative, 27–29
   negative, 24
   outdated language and, 32
   tentative, 25–27
   unkind, 29–31
   whining, 33–36
topic sentence, 15, 77

United States, 198
   U.S., USA, 198

verbs
   active versus passive, 45–51
   agreement of, with subject, 128–145
   turned into nouns, 74–75
vertical lists, to test parallel form, 115–119
versus, 198
very, 158
virgule or slash, 168–169
vowel sound, overuse of, 88

Wall Street Journal, 8
which, that, 63–64
whining tone, avoiding, 33–36
white space, 76–78
who, whom, 102–103
whoever/whomever, 103–106
will, shall, 63
-wise, 66
with, 134
word programs, limitations, 81, 221–226

word order, 21–22
word(s)
  concrete versus abstract,
    173–178
  repetition of, 108–111
  turned into verbs, 65–66
  using correct, 52–67
  using nonoffensive,
    120–127
  varying length of, 80
  versus numerals, 212–220
would, 25
would have … would have, 144
writer-centered writing, 1–5,
  9–11

year date, written without
  commas, 216–217
you, 9, 11
you-focused writing, 1–5,
  9–11
yrs, 199